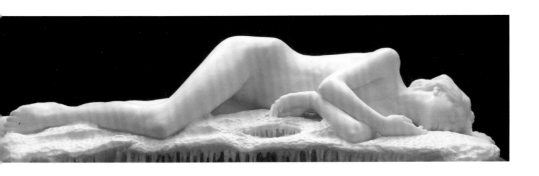

Lady
Lever
Art
Gallery

Published by
National Museums Liverpool
127 Dale Street
Liverpool
L2 2JH

© National Museums Liverpool, 2013

Revised and reprinted, 2017

ISBN 978-1-902700-49-6

Designed by Val Evans Design
www.valevans.com

Whilst we make every effort to ensure that the pieces featured in this book are always on display, there may be occasions when works are not available to the public, eg if they are on outward loan or are undergoing conservation work. Please contact the Gallery before travelling to see a particular piece.

Contents

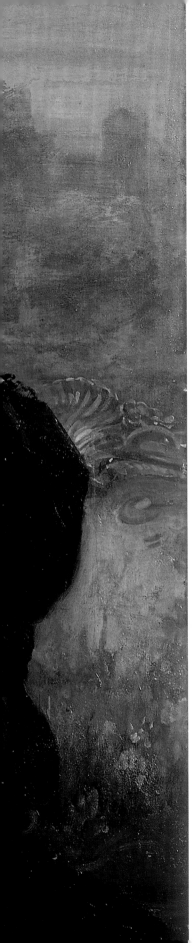

Foreword

The Lady Lever Art Gallery was founded in 1922 by William Hesketh Lever, later the first Viscount Leverhulme, to house what he regarded as the best of his personal art collection. The Gallery was originally run as a charitable trust but in 1978 it was transferred to the public domain, first under the stewardship of the Merseyside County Council and from 1986 to National Museums and Galleries on Merseyside, now National Museums Liverpool. The Gallery was granted national status in recognition of the outstanding quality of its collections.

Lever established the Gallery in his factory village of Port Sunlight, as a cultural and educational resource for his workforce and the public at large. He did so because of his conviction that art could be an inspiring and stimulating influence. As Lever himself said at the opening of the Gallery:

'Art has always been to me a stimulating influence; it has always taught me without upbraiding me; elevated me without humbling me; and appealed to me because of this fact, that only the best and truest in art survives... Art can be to everyone an inspiration.'

The inspirational quality of art is a belief shared by National Museums Liverpool. We hope this guidebook will help our many visitors to understand and enjoy the collections.

We would like to thank all those who have contributed to the various editions of the guidebook: Xanthe Brooke, Robin Emmerson, Alex Kidson, Emma Martin, David Moffat, Edward Morris, Gina Muskett, Alyson Pollard, Andrew Renton, Pauline Rushton and Lucy Wood for selecting works and writing the text, David Flower, Colin Jackson and Clare Bates for photography, Val Evans for her design work and Karen Miller for editing and seeing the book through to production.

The descendants of the first Lord Leverhulme take an active and positive interest in the Gallery. The Trustees of National Museums Liverpool greatly value this association and would like to thank them for their continuing and generous support of this most personal and individual of galleries.

David Fleming
Director, National Museums Liverpool

*Mrs William Hesketh Lever,
later 1st Lady Lever,* 1896

Luke Fildes (1844-1927)
British
Oil on canvas, 119 x 84.3 cm
Presented to the Gallery by the 3rd Viscount
Leverhulme, 1980; inv. no. LL 3115

Sandra Penketh
Director of Art Galleries,
National Museums Liverpool

Introduction:
The creation of the Lady Lever Art Gallery

The Lady Lever Art Gallery - both the building and its collections - was the creation of one man, William Hesketh Lever, 1st Viscount Leverhulme (1851-1925), founder of Lever Brothers and the model village of Port Sunlight, and art collector on a scale unmatched in Britain since his death.

William Lever was born in Bolton, Lancashire, the son of a wholesale grocer. The family were Congregationalists, and the nonconformist ethos of self-discipline and entrepreneurship was profoundly influential on Lever's whole life and career. He left school to join the family firm at the age of 16, becoming a salaried partner at 21, and devoted his energies to expanding the business in the 1870s and early '80s. It was only in 1884 that he decided to focus on selling a single product, household soap, to which he was drawn not by any technical interest in its manufacture - at this stage the actual production was contracted out - but by its potential for marketing in pre-wrapped bars under a brand name. (Until then soap had been sold like cheese, cut to order for each customer from a large block.) Two years later he began to manufacture soap himself and established the new firm of Lever Brothers for the purpose; due to illness his brother and nominal partner, James Darcy Lever, played little part in the business. Initially Lever took over an existing soap works in Warrington, but by 1888 he had outgrown the factory's capacity, and decided to build a new factory on a much larger scale. He chose a greenfield site on the Wirral shore of the Mersey, to build not only the factory but the adjacent village to house his employees, and named the whole complex Port Sunlight after his most successful brand of soap.

Lever's career as a serious collector also stems from this moment. In the late 1880s he began to buy pictures from the summer exhibitions of the Royal Academy, specifically for the purpose of advertising Sunlight Soap. His advertisement reproducing WP Frith's *The New Frock*, bought at the 1889 summer exhibition, involved him in a notorious argument with the artist about the ethics of this use (or abuse) of art (fig. 7). It also marked Lever's entry into the London art market. At the same time his move to the house Thornton Manor, which he immediately set about enlarging, created opportunities for display on a larger scale than his previous houses had allowed (fig. 6). He himself always pointed to a pair of Derby biscuit porcelain figures (fig. 2), acquired in the late 1870s for his house in Wigan, as the starting point of his collections, but it was the Port Sunlight venture that opened up grander possibilities of buying works of art, and it was only in the mid-1890s that Lever began collecting on a significant scale.

Fig. 1   The Main Hall of the Lady Lever Art Gallery, about 1922

Lever's development from a casual art buyer to a serious collector was accelerated by his encounter, in about 1896, with James Orrock (1829-1913), artist, collector and part-time dealer, and a passionate advocate of British art. Orrock had trained as a surgeon-dentist in Edinburgh, and practised for some years in Nottingham before moving to London in about 1866 to become a full-time artist. He began buying works of art while in Nottingham, but in London he became a major collector, primarily of English 18th- and early 19th-century pictures and watercolours, of 18th-century English furniture and of 17th- and 18th-century Chinese porcelain (which he evidently regarded as an integral aspect of English baroque and Georgian taste). At the same time he campaigned for the establishment of a national gallery of British art - both fine and decorative - which he considered grossly neglected by the artistic establishment of his day.

Lever now took up Orrock's cause, and began to collect in a much more focused way, embracing the same periods as Orrock in English and Chinese art; and bought Orrock's own collection in its entirety on three occasions, in 1904, 1910 and 1912. But he rapidly outstripped Orrock as a collector, in both the quality and quantity of his collections, and the scope of his interests. As a collector of 18th-century British portraits and landscapes - of which only a small proportion came to the Lady Lever Art Gallery - Lever was rivalled only by the great American collectors such as Henry Huntington and J Pierpont Morgan; and in his purchase of English 17th- and 18th-century furniture he remains unequalled by any other private collector.

Fig. 2   Lever's house in Wigan, about 1877-80. On the chimneypiece is the pair of Derby biscuit figures that he regarded as the foundation-pieces of his art collection

In addition Lever became an important collector of Victorian pictures, especially by the Pre-Raphaelites and their successors, and by classical artists such as Leighton and Alma-Tadema; his earliest acquisitions in this field (in 1893-4) probably predating his acquaintance with Orrock. He was also an early and prominent collector and patron of such sculptors as Edward Onslow Ford and Francis Derwent Wood, adherents of the anti-classical 'New Sculpture' movement. And in about 1900 he began to collect English 17th- and 18th-century embroideries, one of the first generation of British and American collectors to take an interest in this subject.

His collecting of Wedgwood began with the acquisition in 1905 of the highly distinguished collection formed by the 1st Lord Tweedmouth (1820-94). Lever often bought in bulk from established collections - starting with his first block purchase from Orrock in 1904 - to enhance both the size and the stature of his own collection. His extensive purchases at the 1917 sale of Greek vases and Roman sculpture originally assembled by Thomas Hope (1769-1831) turned Lever's moderate holdings into a major collection of antiquities. He made similar large-scale, and in some instances wholesale, purchases to build up his holdings of Chinese art and parts of his 'Museum' collection.

Fig. 3   The exterior of Thornton Manor, about 1903. Photographer: Bedford Lemere. Reproduced by permission of Historic England Archive.

From about 1902 Lever began to place parts of his collection on public display in Port Sunlight. In the same year he opened Hall-i'-th'-Wood, a timber-framed house near his home town of Bolton, as a folk museum, furnished with 16th- and 17th-century oak furniture. His private, and at that point more prestigious, collection also gained wider publicity after his purchase in 1904 of a house in Hampstead, The Hill, to which he at once decanted the majority of the works of art then at Thornton Manor. Two years later his company suffered commercial reverses which drastically reduced his purchasing power, but on recovery Lever was more than ever committed to public display of his collections. In 1911 he opened two museums: Rivington Hall, a largely 18th-century house on his estate in Lancashire; and Hulme Hall in Port Sunlight, originally built as the women employees' canteen but now adapted as a museum and art gallery and filled chiefly with the collections recently bought from Orrock.

The limitations of Hulme Hall as an art gallery were shown up by Lever's 1913 purchase of a number of grand Victorian pictures at the sale of George McCulloch's collection, including Leighton's vast *Daphnephoria*. This was evidently the final catalyst

Fig. 4   The opening of the Lady Lever Art Gallery, 16 December 1922. Princess Beatrice is opening the south door, with Lever (hat in hand), standing behind. Reproduced with kind permission of Unilever from an original in Unilever Archives.

in Lever's decision to establish a new, purpose-built public gallery in Port Sunlight Village, suitable for the display of these imposing works; the *Daphnephoria* still dominates the north end of the main hall for which it was always intended (fig. 5). The first plans for the Gallery were laid in June 1913, and after his wife's death the following month Lever decided to name the Gallery in her memory. (He paid her another tribute when he was made a peer four years later by adding her maiden name of Hulme to his own surname to form his title; at her death he was already a baronet, so she was Lady Lever but never became Lady Leverhulme.)

Lever's architects were the Warrington firm of William & Segar Owen - who had been involved from the outset in the creation of Port Sunlight Village - but Lever himself exercised close control over every aspect of the building. It is in the classical style fostered by the Paris Ecole des Beaux Arts, a striking contrast to the English style of the Village housing; but it is likely that American architecture (on which Beaux Arts classicism was a powerful influence) provided the direct inspiration for Lever's choice. Beneath the Portland stone cladding, and the interior plasterwork, the Gallery is constructed of reinforced concrete, an early example of the use of this new material for a prominent building in Britain.

Lever personally selected every work of art from his private collection that was to come to the new Gallery. But its foundation also influenced his pattern of buying, for he now began to acquire pictures and objects specifically for display in the planned Gallery. Although he had probably thought of founding a public art gallery from an early date (perhaps soon after taking up Orrock's campaign on behalf of British art), this conscious separation of his private and public collections marks a new departure. Partly it was simply a matter of scale: just as he had no room in his houses to do justice to the McCulloch collection, so he never intended the great state bed from Stowe (p. 60), bought in 1921, to be seen anywhere other than the Gallery. Partly, Lever understood the need to appeal to a wide public audience, and so he bought part of Sir Herbert Graystone's collection of armour in 1923, explaining to one of his dealers, 'I wanted these more as an attraction for those at the Gallery who... do not particularly admire pictures, statuary, etc. I have to cater for all tastes at the Gallery.' More significantly, he weighted his selection of pictures in favour of Victorian works, especially narrative subjects, with much less emphasis on 18th-century painting than in his private collection. His instinct that the former would have more popular appeal has proved justified to this day.

However, Lever was also concerned to make his public collection more representative, perhaps seeking variety for its own sake, but also aiming to give a more informative picture of developments in certain key areas. He acquired some Elizabethan and Jacobean furniture, to complement the much more numerous later Stuart and Georgian pieces; he added Chinese hardstones and cloisonné enamels to his very large collection of Chinese porcelain; and he bought Greek and Roman antiquities presumably to underpin the classical basis of the collection as a whole.

The growth of the collections of fine and decorative art took place at the expense of Lever's so-called 'Museum' collection, which had been an important element in his original conception of the Gallery. Its nucleus, consisting mainly of ethnographic items, had been publicly displayed in Port Sunlight since at least 1903. Later additions to the 'Museum' section included most of the Greek and Roman antiquities and a collection of objects associated with Freemasonry, all of which were bought specifically for the Gallery. However, the 'Art' collection expanded to fill the available space, leaving little room for any 'Museum' material (with the exception of some antique sculpture).

The Lady Lever Art Gallery was eventually opened in 1922 by Princess Beatrice (youngest daughter of Queen Victoria), progress having been delayed by the First World War. (fig. 4) Lever continued adding to the collection for the remaining three years of his life. After his death in May 1925 the parts of his collection that had not been selected for the Gallery (approximately half) were dispersed in a series of sales, altogether lasting 45 days, in both London and New York. But despite the fact that when he died Lever was still sorting his private collection from this public bequest, the best of his extraordinary accumulation of works of art had already been placed in the Gallery. It remains, notwithstanding the dedication to his wife, a remarkable memorial to his taste and philanthropy.

St. Ursula before the King of the Huns, about 1400-10

Spanish (Valencia)

Tempera on panel, 116.5 x 64 cm

Purchased by Lever, 1919;
inv. no. LL 3428 (WHL 3752c)

This is one of four panels from the lower half of an altarpiece illustrating the story of the martyrdom of St Ursula and her 11,000 female followers, who were massacred by the King of the Huns at Cologne. The four upper panels are in the Prado Museum, Madrid, and all originally came from an altarpiece in the Dominican church of San Pablo in Palencia, Castile. It was probably the highly decorative nature of the paintings, with their skilled use of punched work and tooling on the gold background and the wealth of detail in the dress, textiles and patterned flooring that attracted Lever to these panels, unusual in his collection for being foreign and medieval.

Paintings and Sculpture

By the time of his death in 1925, Lord Leverhulme owned thousands of paintings, drawings and sculptures. The vast majority of these works were British, reflecting his long-held wish to create, in the shape of the Lady Lever Art Gallery, a public gallery of British art that would present a more rounded picture of the achievements of the national school than could be found in any existing institution at that date. The precise flavour of the gallery, in which fine and decorative arts would be displayed together, and in which a select group of foreign works would contrast with and set off the 'national' characteristics of the bulk of the contents, closely reflected the views and tastes of Lever's friend James Orrock, the collector and dealer who, on three occasions between 1904 and his death in 1913, sold Lever his own collections in their entirety. The strengths (and weaknesses) in the Gallery's late 18th- and early 19th-century British holdings in particular are a testimony to his influence.

By the canons of his time, Lever's British pictures offered a rich and representative survey of the greatness of the national school. The collection did not entirely neglect 17th- and early 18th-century art, but it concentrated heavily on the period from about 1750 to 1900 when British painting was widely perceived to have reached and indeed exceeded in stature that of other European countries. Within that period, Lever concentrated further on three areas where such claims might carry particular weight. The first featured the foundation and rise of the Royal Academy. Concentrating on the grand-manner portraiture of Joshua Reynolds and the Italian landscapes of Richard Wilson, Lever built up a core of paintings that witnessed British artists, while sustaining the favourite national genres of the portrait and the landscape, for the first time engaging maturely with the mainstream classical tradition of European art. This cluster of works, whose highlights are Reynolds'

Duchess of Hamilton and Wilson's *Landscape with Diana and Callisto,* both from the end of the 1750s, was set in relief by a series of less imposing, but at the time equally fashionable, Georgian pictures: chiefly portraits by Gainsborough, Romney and Hoppner, and the rustic scenes of Morland and Wheatley. (By contrast, the group of four enamel paintings by George Stubbs, which from today's vantage point are much the most remarkable early British pictures in the collection, probably appealed to Lever largely as unusual examples of Wedgwood ware.)

The second area very fully represented in Lever's collection was the golden age of British landscape painting, roughly from 1800 to 1850. Constable and Turner, with their altogether new intensity of response to the landscape and the forces of nature, were then as now regarded as the dominant figures of this era; but almost equally significant for Lever were the landscapists whose greatest contribution had been in the medium of watercolour. James Orrock, himself an accomplished watercolourist, was a proponent of the since widely-held view that perfecting the watercolour was the British School's most significant contribution to the history of Western art, and he sold Lever many examples by a canon of key figures, notably David Cox, Peter de Wint, William Henry Hunt and George Barret junior.

A contemporary of these artists, working in a very different tradition, was William Etty, a favourite artist of Orrock and Lever alike. Etty's mastery as a colourist, and the decorative properties of his rich canvases, were probably the main attraction for both of them; but Lever's taste for Etty is suggestive in further ways. On the one hand, as his collection of later 19th-century paintings and more especially sculpture indicates, Lever was very far from shy of the nude figure (the mastery of which lay at the heart of all Academic art). On the other, Etty seems to have answered in Lever an almost compulsive collector's urge in some sense to corner a particular supply: an impulse recognisable in his approach to a number of other artists, which seems intimately bound up with his instincts as a manufacturer and businessman.

The third key area, which dominates the collection, was Victorian art. It was in this field that Lever first began to collect seriously, independently of Orrock's influence, and he continued to do so even after developing other interests. In the late 1880s he started acquiring contemporary, and relatively minor, British paintings for use in advertisements for Sunlight Soap (fig. 7), which explains the number of girls in white frocks, salubrious family gatherings and scenes featuring washing and bathing still to be found in the Gallery. But by the early 1890s he was buying the work of Frederic Leighton and, a little later, of JE Millais, who together with Etty remained his favourite artists throughout his life.

Many of Lever's most important Victorian pictures came from the Christie's sale in 1913 of the collection of George McCulloch (1848-1907), the greatest single private collection of Victorian and Edwardian paintings ever formed. Born in Glasgow, McCulloch made his fortune in Australia, where he emigrated in 1883 to run a sheep-farming station, but discovered and exploited a silver mine at Broken Hill, the immense success of which enabled him to start collecting. In 1892 he returned to live in London, and a few years later built himself a new house in Queen's Gate to accommodate his expanding collection. At his posthumous sale of 1913, Lever was by far the most notable buyer, securing Leighton's *Daphnephoria* and *Garden of the Hesperides,* Millais' *A Dream of the Past: Sir Isumbras at the Ford* and *Lingering Autumn,* as well as major works by lesser artists, such as Luke Fildes,

Henry Moore and JM Swan; and it is no coincidence that he decided to commission the Lady Lever Art Gallery only a few weeks afterwards.

Until the McCulloch sale the majority of Lever's Victorian acquisitions had been contemporary or near-contemporary works: a policy he continued with, for example, the acquisition of two important late works by JW Waterhouse in 1916 and 1917. But after the Gallery's inception he concentrated mainly on assembling a representative collection of mid- and late Victorian art. The major figures of the Pre-Raphaelite movement are all present: Holman Hunt's uncompromisingly realistic masterpieces, *The Scapegoat* and *May Morning on Magdalen Tower,* contrasting with the more 'aesthetic' works of Rossetti and his younger associate Burne-Jones, while social realism is represented by Herkomer's *The Last Muster.* Lever also selected a few works by his friends: landscapes by Alfred East and David Murray, and Luke Fildes' *An Al-fresco Toilette,* perhaps the grandest scene from everyday Venetian life in late Victorian art.

Lever's taste in sculpture was more progressive: personal friendships - with Onslow Ford and Goscombe John - probably played a larger part and he became the single most important patron of the 'New Sculpture'. This movement brought a new poetic realism into British sculpture with a wider range of techniques, of subject matter and of pose, and its highly imaginative bronzes complement the mythic masterpieces of Burne-Jones, Rossetti, Waterhouse and Leighton. Lever's deep commitment to 18th-century classicism and especially to Victorian high art makes the Lady Lever Art Gallery one of the most outstanding and distinctive displays of British paintings and sculpture ever assembled by a single collector.

Fig. 7   Lever's 1890 advertisement for Sunlight Soap using Frith's *The New Frock.* Reproduced with kind permission of Unilever from an original in Unilever Archives.

Fig. 6   The Music Room at Thornton Manor, about 1903. Among the pictures hanging on the end wall are Millais' *The Black Brunswickers,* Leighton's *Fatidica,* and *Napoleon Reading his Letter of Abdication* by George Richmond; on the left wall hangs Romney's *Mrs Oliver,* flanked by two Hoppner portraits, *The Earl of Moira* and *Lady Elizabeth Howard* (see p. 25). All of these are now in the Lady Lever Art Gallery. Photographer: Bedford Lemere. Reproduced by permission of Historic England Archive.

Bust of Ferdinando de' Medici,
about 1700

Giovacchino Fortini (1671-1736)

Italian (Florence)

Marble, 139 (including base) x 90.3 x 59.5 cm

Purchased by Lever, 1922; inv. no. LL 203
(X 4168)

Prince Ferdinando de' Medici of Tuscany (1633-1713) was a great patron of the arts in Florence, with a particular fondness for sculpture. His emblem, lightning striking through clouds, has been carved into his breastplate in the form of a shield, and the related motto, ET LUCET ET TERRET ('It casts both light and terror'), is on the base. Fortini was known for his tomb and church sculpture as well as being an accomplished sculptor of portrait busts and medals, and paid subtle attention to finely worked detail and textural distinctions.

Landscape with Diana and Callisto, about 1757

Richard Wilson (1713-82)

British

Oil on canvas, 103 x 139 cm

Purchased by Lever, 1904;
inv. no. LL 3122 (WHL 641)

The painting, one of several known versions of the subject by Wilson, may have been executed during the artist's stay in Italy between 1752 and 1757. It would have been intended for purchase by an aristocratic collector making the Grand Tour. It is a view of Lake Nemi, a beauty spot not far from Rome and a site familiar to readers of the classics for its association with the goddess Diana. The lake was known as Diana's mirror and there was a shrine to her in the groves above the shore. Wilson alludes to this by representing in the foreground the story of Diana and Callisto from Ovid's *Metamorphoses.* The goddess has just discovered her handmaiden's pregnancy and is banishing her: Callisto's child will be the forefather of the Arcadian people. The calm lucidity and order of Wilson's design consciously recall French classical landscapes of the 17th century by Gaspar Dughet and Claude Lorrain.

*Elizabeth Gunning, Duchess of Hamilton and
Duchess of Argyll,* 1760

Joshua Reynolds (1723-92)

British

Oil on canvas, 238.5 x 147.5 cm

Purchased by Lever from the Hamilton Palace
sale, 1919; inv. no. LL 3126 (WHL 4093)

One of Reynolds' greatest essays in the grand manner, this
portrait was shown at the first-ever Society of Artists exhibition
held in London in 1760. It was clearly intended to display his
powers and his theory of portraiture. The sitter, a famous Irish
beauty, had married the 6th Duke of Hamilton in 1752; recently
widowed at the time of this portrait, she was shortly to marry
John Campbell, the future 5th Duke of Argyll. Reynolds portrays
her in peeress's robes, but the rest of her costume and her
features are idealised, giving her something of the air of an
antique sculpture. The doves and the relief sculpture of the
Judgement of Paris on the left are allusions to the goddess Venus,
and are devices typical of Reynolds' intellectual and elevated
brand of portraiture.

Anne Duchess of Cumberland, about 1780

Thomas Gainsborough (1727-88)

British

Oil on canvas, 76.5 x 63.5 cm

Purchased by Lever, 1920; inv. no. LL 3140 (WHL 4242)

Lever bought this fine example of Gainsborough's later manner as a
portrait of Princess Augusta, daughter of George III. She, however, was
only a girl when most of Gainsborough's portraits of the Royal Family
were undertaken, and the sitter's features strongly resemble those of
Anne Duchess of Cumberland, a previously-married commoner who
controversially became the wife of the King's brother in 1771. Horace
Walpole described her 'with eyelashes a yard long, a coquette beyond
measure and as artful as Cleopatra'. Gainsborough painted her, always
sympathetically, on several occasions, and this work combines brilliance
with intimacy and tenderness.

Lady Emma Hamilton as a Bacchante, probably painted in 1792

Élisabeth Vigée Le Brun (1755-1842)

French

Oil on canvas, 132.5cm x 105.5 cm

Purchased by Lever from Thomas Agnew and Sons , 1903;
inv. no. LL 3527 (WHL 712)

Vigée Le Brun is best known for her female neo-classical costume portraits. As painter and friend of Queen Marie Antoinette she fled France during the French revolution in 1789, fearing that her closeness to the royal family placed her in danger. During her stay in Naples in the early 1790s she met Emma Hamilton and painted her four times. Emma, originally from the Wirral, married the much older Sir William Hamilton, Ambassador to Naples in 1791. As a well known society hostess Emma became famous for her part dance and part performance entertainments, known as 'Attitudes.' In this painting, she is dressed as a Bacchante, a female follower of the wine god Bacchus, with vine leaves tucked into a red head band. She is shown dancing with a tambourine. The smoking volcano Vesuvius, near Naples, is seen in the background.

Mrs Peter Beckford, 1782

Joshua Reynolds (1723-92)

British

Oil on canvas, 239 x 147 cm

Purchased by Lever from the Hamilton Palace
sale, 1919; inv no. LL 3125 (WHL 4094)

This full-length portrait is characteristic of the works by which Reynolds represented himself, as its President, in the Royal Academy's exhibitions of the 1780s. The sitter, wife of a Dorset gentleman, was of a delicate constitution and Reynolds portrays her making a libation (a drink offering) to the Greek goddess of health, Hygeia, whose emblem was a snake. At the time the portrait was painted Louisa Beckford was in the throes of an affair with her husband's celebrated cousin, William Beckford, author of the famous Gothic novel *Vathek;* and Reynolds' conception, with its gloomy, smoke-filled atmosphere and elaborate play of light and shadow, may owe something to Beckford's newly-fashionable literary and aesthetic image.

Self-Portrait, 1782
George Stubbs (1724-1806)
British
Enamel on Wedgwood earthenware plaque, 93 x 71 cm
Purchased by Lever from the Tweedmouth collection, 1905; inv. no. LL 3684 (H 374)

This is one of a handful of surviving enamels which Stubbs painted on ceramic plaques manufactured by Josiah Wedgwood. Stubbs devoted considerable energy to experimenting with and gradually perfecting this new medium, which he believed to be more durable than oil painting on canvas. He exhibited a group of enamels, of which this was one, at the Royal Academy in 1782; but other artists did not respond to them as enthusiastically as both he and Wedgwood had hoped. Acquired almost incidentally as part of Lord Tweedmouth's Wedgwood collection (see p. 83), this oval was perhaps Lever's most remarkable single purchase of an 18th-century British painting. To complement it he later bought its three companions, now in the Gallery.

(see p. 83)

Sarah Rodbard, 1784
George Romney (1734-1802)
British
Oil on canvas, 236 x 152 cm
Purchased by Lever, 1903; inv. no. LL 3539 (WHL 50)

In 1784, when he painted this outstanding full-length, Romney was London's most fashionable portrait painter. He avoided the formality and intellectual pretension of his rival, Joshua Reynolds, in favour of a mood of relaxed elegance, which he achieved through assured, flowing draughtsmanship and restrained colour. Sarah Rodbard was 19 at the time of the portrait; two years later she became the wife of Major (later General Sir Eyre) Coote. Lever's purchase of this work for the high price of £12,000 assured him celebrity status as a collector of Georgian portraiture.

Cephalus and Aurora, 1790

John Flaxman (1755-1826)

British

Marble, 146 x 102 x 67 cm

Purchased by Lever at the Hope Heirlooms sale, 1917, then presented to the Gallery by the 2nd Viscount Leverhulme, 1929; inv. no. LL 713 (LS 5)

The story of Cephalus, retold in Ovid's *Metamorphoses,* was popular among artists in the 17th and 18th centuries. Flaxman represents the moment in which the youth, after resisting her advances, finally yields to the amorous Aurora, Greek goddess of the dawn. It was one of the artist's first major sculptures and was made in Rome, where he had travelled to study the antique: a trip financed by his work for Josiah Wedgwood. The sculpture was purchased from the celebrated collector Thomas Hope, one of the prime movers of neo-classical taste; it formed the centrepiece of the famous 'Star Room' (decorated throughout with emblems of dawn and the retreating night) at his London house in Duchess Street. Lever purchased it with many of his antique sculptures at the Hope Heirlooms Sale.

HAY CARTING
G. STUBBS R.A. 1795

Haycarting, 1795

George Stubbs (1724-1806)

British

Enamel on Wedgwood earthenware plaque, 77 x 105 cm

Purchased by Lever, 1915; inv. no. LL 3683 (WHL 2180)

This is one of three enamels which Stubbs executed in the mid-1790s on the theme of haymaking. Although they are repetitions, with slight variations, of subjects which he had painted in oils over a decade previously, they can be seen as the apogee of his work in enamel, limpid in colour and masterly in design. The figures, carefully studied in relation to each other, have a statuesque, arresting quality which elevates them from the type of common rural labourer into the individual heroes of some frieze from antiquity.

The Judgement of Paris, 1825-6

William Etty (1787-1849)

British

Oil on canvas, 183 x 277 cm

Purchased by Lever, 1911; inv. no. LL 3588 (WHL 642)

Paris, the son of King Priam, hands the apple to Aphrodite, goddess of love, in preference to her rivals, and sets in train the events that will lead to the Trojan Wars. Etty, who excelled with subjects suited to the female nude, was one of the few British artists of the period to enjoy success as a history painter and this was one of his grandest works. It was commissioned by the 4th Earl of Darnley and exhibited at the Royal Academy in 1826. Etty's sources included the famous engraving of Raphael's *Judgement of Paris* by Marcantonio Raimondi and Flaxman's illustrations to the *Iliad,* but his rich colour is indebted to Venetian art, above all that of his mentor Titian.

*Lady Elizabeth Howard,
later Duchess of Rutland,* 1798

John Hoppner (1758-1810)

British

Oil on canvas, 127 x 101.5 cm

Purchased by Lever, 1897;
inv. no. LL 3128 (WHL 73)

The sitter, 18 years old at the date
of this portrait, was the daughter of
Frederick, 5th Earl of Carlisle, a member
of the Whig aristocracy in the circle
of the Prince Regent. Through the
influence of this group of patrons,
Hoppner established himself as a
natural successor to Joshua Reynolds
in the 1790s, developing Reynolds'
manner, with its concentration on warm,
harmonious colour, tonal subtlety and
a richly-worked surface. Although less
brilliant and adventurous than his great
rival Lawrence, Hoppner at his best - as
here - achieved portraits of genuine
poetry and feeling.

Dudley, about 1832

Joseph Mallord William Turner (1775-1851)

British

Watercolour and bodycolour on paper, 28 x 43 cm

Purchased by Lever, 1919; inv. no. LL 3923 (WHL 4030)

Turner's view incorporates both the antiquity of the hillside market town, with its
castle and church, and the industrial life of a great new centre for the manufacture
of glass and iron. The harsh glare of the forges and the brilliant light reflected in
the water of the foreground canal impart a supernatural quality to this spectacular
and sublime vision of the Industrial Revolution, suddenly erupting within England's
ancient landscape. This watercolour, made for the series *Picturesque views in
England and Wales,* shows Turner's ability to transform an ordinary landscape and
everyday life into a splendid panorama of light and colour.

Cottage at East Bergholt, about 1833
John Constable (1776-1837)
British
Oil on canvas, 87.5 x 112 cm
Purchased by Lever, 1904; inv. no. LL 3120 (WHL 557)

The strips of canvas added to both sides suggest that Constable made this sketch to work out the composition for a proposed exhibition picture. The title is an invention: though the scene is reminiscent of many of his Suffolk landscapes, and combines motifs from earlier paintings, the specific viewpoint has not been identified and may have been imaginary. At the time of its acquisition by Lever the work was notorious: the subject of a celebrated debate over Constable forgeries. Today it is prized as one of the artist's finest late works, a tour-de-force of palette-knife painting and an image of brooding, almost mystical power.

The Falls of the Clyde, about 1840

Joseph Mallord William Turner (1775-1851)

British

Oil on canvas, 89 x 119.5 cm

Purchased by Lever, 1923; inv. no. LL 3584 (WHL 4708)

One of a group of late and experimental oils, not intended for
public exhibition, in which Turner freely reworked subjects he
had first treated decades before. The source for this canvas was
a large watercolour he had completed in 1802, now in the Walker
Art Gallery, Liverpool. Situated on the upper Clyde near Lanark,
the falls had become an attraction for tourists at the end of the
18th century when they had been painted by a number of artists.
Turner's abiding fascination with the effects of strong light, here
playing on the spray of cascading water, converts a picturesque
scene into a profound expression of the elemental forces and
primary colours of nature.

The Scapegoat, 1854

William Holman Hunt (1827-1910)

British

Oil on canvas, 87 x 139.8 cm

Purchased by Lever, 1923; inv. no. LL 3623 (WHL 4706)

Each year on the Day of Atonement, the High Priest in the Temple of Jerusalem cast a goat out into the desert as a symbolic act of expiation for the sins of the Israelites. The custom is described in the Old Testament, but Hunt linked it to the New Testament, making the animal into a symbol of Christ, who took upon himself the sins of the world: the scarlet thread around its horns, referred to in the Talmud, suggests the crown of thorns. The goat stares out accusingly, giving the picture an uncomfortable yet memorable emotional force. Hunt travelled to Palestine to search out authentic settings for his Biblical scenes, and this landscape was painted by the desolate shores of the Dead Sea, at a spot thought to be the site of the city of Sodom. The vivid colours and sharply painted details are characteristic of Pre-Raphaelite naturalism.

A Dream of the Past: Sir Isumbras at the Ford, 1857

John Everett Millais (1829-96)

British

Oil on canvas, 125.5 x 171.5 cm

Purchased by Lever from the George McCulloch sale, 1913; inv. no. LL 3625 (WHL 19)

An example of the Pre-Raphaelites' interest in subjects about medieval chivalry:
an ancient knight in golden armour is carrying the children of a poor woodcutter
across a river. Sir Isumbras is a character from a 14th-century English romance, but
this incident does not occur in the poem. It may have been invented by Millais' friend
the art critic Tom Taylor, who wrote a fake medieval verse explaining the story.
Many critics thought the horse was too big, and it was repainted several times, but
the landscape background was much admired. Its loose and fluid handling, which
contrasts with the artist's earlier more detailed landscape style, captures the fleeting
effect of twilight, with a solemnity perhaps intended to suggest a deeper, spiritual
meaning about the end of the knight's quest and the transience of worldly deeds.

Spring (Apple Blossoms), 1859

John Everett Millais (1829-96)

British

Oil on canvas, 110.5 x 45.7 cm

Purchased by Lever, 1920, then purchased from the 3rd Viscount Leverhulme for the Lady Lever Art Gallery, 1986, with the assistance of the National Heritage Memorial Fund; inv. no. LL 3624 (WHL 4114)

Though known for his historical narrative paintings such as *Sir Isumbras at the Ford* and *The Black Brunswickers,* Millais at about the same time painted a small number of modern dress pictures without specific stories. They were 'mood' pictures intended to awaken 'the deepest religious reflection', to quote the artist's own words. The girls, relaxing in an orchard of spring blossom, are eating curds and cream, but the underlying theme is the transience of youth and beauty, expressed in the fragile bloom of adolescence, the wild flowers and the changing seasons; and the inevitability of death, whose presence is indicated by the scythe on the right. This type of picture, showing contemplative figures seated in an idyllic landscape, goes back to the *fête champêtre* paintings of Titian and Giorgione, and anticipates the figure compositions of dreamy young women painted by Whistler in the 1860s.

The Bathers, 1865-9
Frederick Walker (1840-75)
British
Oil on canvas, 92.7 x 214.7 cm
Purchased by Lever, 1918;
inv. no. LL 3143 (WHL 3420)

This painting seems to show just a few boys drying themselves after bathing in the Thames near Cookham where the artist painted his subject on the spot to ensure accuracy of tone and colour. In fact, Walker has borrowed many of his poses from famous Greek and Roman sculptures and his subject from a famous cartoon by Michelangelo, also called *The Bathers,* representing an incident from a battle. Some contemporary critics found the final result close to parody but the classical grandeur and grace achieved by Walker were a remarkable achievement for an artist not yet 30 years old.

The Black Brunswickers, 1860
John Everett Millais (1829-96)

Oil on canvas, 104 x 68.5 cm
Purchased by William Hesketh Lever in 1898, inv. no. LL 3643

The Black Brunswickers were formed in 1809 by Frederick William, Duke of Brunswick (1771-1815), nephew of George III. They were known for their black uniforms and distinctive death's-head cap badge. On 16 June 1815 they fought Napoleon's troops in the battle of Quatre Bras at Waterloo and suffered severe losses, including the death of their Commander-in-Chief, the Duke of Brunswick. Two days later they fought in the Battle of Waterloo. Millais gives a taste of the drama to come by adding a framed print of Napoleon in the top left corner of the painting.

For this picture of a young German officer and his English sweetheart parting on the eve of the momentous battle Millais used the author Charles Dickens' daughter Kate as a model. To maintain her respectability Kate, and the private from the Life Guards who sat for the officer, modelled for Millais at separate times, using an artist's dummy to stand in for the other figure.

The Beguiling of Merlin, 1872-7

Edward Coley Burne-Jones (1833-98)

British

Oil on canvas, 186 x 111 cm

Purchased by Lever, 1918; inv. no. LL 3121 (WHL 3509)

The story is taken from the Arthurian Legends, which were the artist's favourite subjects. Merlin had fallen in love with Nimue (also called Nimiane, Vivian or Vivien). This enabled her to learn his skills in enchantment and here she is sending Merlin into a deep sleep. Burne-Jones had become infatuated with one of his admirers, Mary Zambaco, in the 1860s, and so the powerful sexual tension in the painting reflected his own situation. The long sinuous lines of her figure and of the hawthorn trees behind still entrance the spectator - as they bewitched Merlin in the legend.

33

Cromwell on his farm, 1873-4
Ford Madox Brown (1821-93)

British

Oil on canvas, 143 x 104.3 cm

Purchased by Lever, 1899; inv. no. LL 3641 (WHL 21)

The future Lord Protector is shown as a Huntingdonshire farmer before his rise to power during the English Civil Wars. Although everyday life on his farm teems obtrusively around him, Cromwell stares prophetically into the future. The symbolism is rich. Cromwell's oak sapling represents his future strength, while the bonfire demonstrates divine wrath at royalist England. Cromwell was one of the great leaders hero-worshipped by Thomas Carlyle, whose writings deeply influenced Brown and inspired this painting; both author and artist profoundly admired Cromwell's political and religious radicalism.

The Daphnephoria, 1874-6
Frederic Leighton (1830-96)

British

Oil on canvas, 231 x 525 cm

Purchased by Lever from the George McCulloch sale, 1913; inv. no. LL 3632 (WHL 1177)

The Daphnephoria was an ancient festival held in honour of Apollo commemorating in particular a Theban victory over the Aeolians. This is the grandest of a group of huge processional pictures on which Leighton's reputation largely rests. His classical vision of the beauty of form, his skill in grouping and arranging his figures and his imagination in conceiving the rich and luxuriant setting make this one of the very few British paintings which can be compared with the great historical and mythological works of 19th-century France and Germany. It was painted for the dining room of his close friend and patron, the banker James Stewart Hodgson, who was compelled to sell it following the first collapse of Barings Bank in 1890.

The Last Muster: Sunday at the Royal Hospital, Chelsea, 1875

Hubert von Herkomer (1849-1914)

British

Oil on canvas, 214.5 x 159 cm

Purchased by Lever, 1923; inv. no. LL 3627 (WHL 4705)

This was painted after the artist had attended a service at the chapel of the Royal Hospital, Chelsea, a home for veteran soldiers ('Chelsea Pensioners') who were unable to support themselves after leaving the army. Herkomer wrote, 'The idea was to make every man tell some different story, to be told by his face, or by the selection of attitude.' The attitude of the central figure, slumped forward, his stick slipping from his grasp, indicates that he has indeed answered 'the last muster'; his neighbour anxiously feels his pulse. Poverty and death were unusual subjects for Victorian painters, who invariably presented them in an ennobling and dignified light. Herkomer had made his name with illustrations of social deprivation in the *Graphic* magazine, and first published a version of this subject in 1871. He then worked it up into this painting, which received high praise at the Royal Academy and went on to win a gold medal at the Paris exhibition of 1878.

The Blessed Damozel, 1875-9

Dante Gabriel Rossetti (1826-82)

British

Oil on canvas, 111 x 82.7 cm, plus
predella 36.5 x 82.8 cm

Purchased by Lever, 1922;
inv. no. LL 3148 (WHL 4391)

This illustrates Rossetti's much earlier poem of about 1850 about a damsel who died young and went to heaven, where she pined for her earthbound lover, waiting for him to die so that they could be reunited. She is depicted as described in the poem's first stanza, leaning from the gold bar of Heaven:

'She had three lilies in her hand, and the stars in her hair were seven.'

Many of Rossetti's paintings of this period feature scenes of unhappy or unconsummated love. There is a larger version of this picture in the Fogg Art Museum, Harvard. Both use the format of a Renaissance altarpiece, with the main scene in a large panel and a smaller predella panel below for the secondary figure.

The Tepidarium, 1881

Lawrence Alma-Tadema (1836-1912)

Dutch

Oil on panel, 24 x 33cm

Purchased by Lever from A and F Pears Ltd.,
1916; inv. no. LL 3130 (WHL 2898)

Alma-Tadema was born in Holland but settled in London, where he achieved great success with his scenes of daily life in ancient times. The tepidarium was the warm Roman bath; the girl holds an ostrich feather and a strigel used for scraping the skin after soaping and oiling it. Alma-Tadema generally contrasts erudite archaeology with aggressively modern figures and attitudes. He was also the most gifted exponent among Victorian painters in rendering exactly textures, surfaces and colours. This combination of realism and learning proved very disconcerting when applied to the nude, and it is surprising that A and F Pears could ever have considered using this painting in a soap advertisement, appropriate for the purpose as it is.

A Maid so Young (Childhood),
1896-7

William Goscombe John (1860-1952)

British

Gilt bronze, 41 (with plinth) x 15 x 18 cm

Presented to the Gallery by Mrs Muriel
Fildes, 1953; inv. no. LL 701

The model for this bust was the sculptor's
young daughter, who presented it to the
Gallery many years later. Children in quiet,
pensive moods had a special appeal to
the artists of the 'New Sculpture', which,
with its poetic realism, was the dominant
force in British sculpture at the end of the
19th century. The strange bonnet adds
a note of fantasy and imagination to the
young face.

Boulter's Lock, Sunday Afternoon, 1882-97

Edward John Gregory (1850-1909)

British

Oil on canvas, 215 x 142 cm

Purchased by Lever from the CJ Galloway sale, 1905; inv. no. LL3149 (WHL33)

Boating on the upper Thames, particularly in the picturesque sections of the river
around Maidenhead where this scene is located, was a national pastime in the late 19th
century. Gregory has painted a panorama of upper middle-class social life: the 'new'
woman energetically paddling her own canoe is contrasted with the young woman in the
foreground with her lap dog delicately holding the tasselled steering ropes; the artist
himself lies back watching the scene at the extreme right, while the other men struggle to
get their boats out of the lock. The very high view-point and the manner in which boats are
cut off by the edge of the painting reflect 'advanced' theories of composition influenced by
Japanese art - rather out of harmony with the very traditional subject-matter.

An Al-fresco Toilette,
1887-9

Samuel Luke Fildes
(1843-1927)

British

Oil on canvas, 173 x 108 cm

Purchased by Lever from the
George McCulloch sale, 1913;
inv. no. LL 3621 (WHL 16)

The Neo-Venetian School was
an international group of artists
painting an idealised version of
the everyday life of working-class
inhabitants of Venice in the 1880s
and 1890s. Fildes briefly belonged
to this school before turning to
portraiture around 1890. Here he
has contrasted the grandeur of
16th- and 17th-century Venetian
palaces with the frivolity of their
late 19th-century tenants. In
fact, the palace was the studio
of the artist's brother-in-law and
the models included his wife and
young son. The artificiality of the
final result may have suggested
to the artist that he should seek
other subjects, although his
command of grouping and pose is
remarkable.

The New Frock, 1889

William Powell Frith (1819-1909)

British

Oil on canvas, 92 x 72 cm

Purchased by Lever from the artist, 1889, then presented to the Gallery by
Lever Brothers, 1983; inv. no. LL 3419

Lever first began to collect paintings in the late 1880s in order to acquire images that
could be incorporated into advertisements for the Sunlight Soap manufactured by his
company. In this painting, the sentimental emphasis on the girl's pride in her appearance
and clothes made it ideal for the purpose, although the artist vigorously protested at
what he saw as the prostitution of his art for commercial purposes (fig. 7, see p. 17).
He had in fact entitled the painting, 'Vanity of vanities, all is vanity', so his message was
exactly the opposite to that insisted on by Lever in his soap advertisements.

May Morning on Magdalen Tower, 1890

William Holman Hunt (1827-1910)

British

Oil on canvas, 154.5 x 200 cm

Purchased by Lever, 1919; inv. no. LL 3599 (WHL 4042)

This shows the ceremony of greeting the sun on May Morning from the top of the tower of Magdalen College, Oxford. Hunt's aim was to create a modern religious subject, linking contemporary Christian worship with ancient times. The ceremony was thought to originate with the Druids, and the inclusion of a Parsee, an Indian sun worshipper, from the Indian Institute at Oxford, further indicates the pantheistic tenor of Hunt's symbolism, which associates the light of the sun, spring flowers, music and boyhood innocence with the Divine force. Hunt also designed the beaten copper frame (made by CR Ashbee's Guild of Handicraft), showing the sun awakening plants and animals into life. The figures are portraits of the President, Fellows and choristers of the college, though some of the boys were not members of the choir but were included for their looks: despite the convincing 'truth to nature' of the scene, Hunt's purpose was primarily symbolic, not realistic.

The Wedding Morning, 1892

John Henry Frederick Bacon (1866-1913)

British

Oil on canvas, 118 x 163 cm

Purchased from the artist 1892; inv. no. LL 3124

This picture shows the influence of French painting and the Newlyn School of Art. Using a scene from the lives of working people, Bacon studies the effects of intense light and shadow in an interior scene. Lever bought this picture when it was first exhibited to use as an advertisement for his Sunlight Soap. In the copy made for the advert, the cup and saucer on the table at the left is replaced by a bar of Sunlight Soap as is the clock on the mantelpiece.

The Garden of the Hesperides, 1891-2

Frederic Leighton (1830-96)

British

Oil on canvas, 169.5 x 169.5 cm

Purchased by Lever from the George McCulloch sale, 1913; inv. no. LL 3139 (WHL 29)

The Hesperides, daughters of Hesperus, the god of evening, protected the golden apples given to Juno or Jupiter on their marriage. They were helped by the dragon, Ladon, who never slept. In due course Hercules killed the dragon and stole the apples but here the artist has selected an idyllic moment of perfect harmony as the Hesperides sing to the sleepless dragon. This harmony is also reflected in the composition of the painting with the long undulating lies of the figures, draperies and animals echoing the circular format of the picture. The flat almost abstract design and the static, emotionless figures are characteristic of many of the artist's late works.

Salammbo, 1899

Maurice Ferrary (1852-1904)

French

Marble and bronze, 272 x 89 x 100.5 cm

Purchased by Lever from the sculptor, 1900; inv. no. LL 205 (TM 401)

Flaubert's great historical novel, *Salammbo,* of 1862 relates that, during the wars between the Carthaginians and the barbarians in the 3rd century BC, Salammbo, the daughter of the Carthaginian leader, 'entwined herself with the genius of her family, with the very religion of her country under its most ancient symbol', that is with the huge snake. With this sacred protection she then went out to the barbarian camp to retrieve the famous veil, the loss of which had caused defeat for the Carthaginians. This subject, widely condemned as indecent even within Flaubert's novel, was very popular with a group of late 19th-century French sculptors preoccupied with erotic and sensual themes.

Snowdrift, 1901

Edward Onslow Ford (1852-1901)

British

Marble, green onyx, lapis lazuli with silver mounts, black
marble, 39.5 x 90.5 x 35.6 cm

Purchased by Lever from the artist's executors, 1911;
inv. no. LL 47 (H 540)

The figure is conceived as a personification of snow, or
perhaps of the spirit of winter, and here, with the coming
of spring, the snow is melting and she is sleeping, or dying.
The sculptor combines intense poetry in the unusual pose
and haunting expression of the girl with direct realism in the
modelling of her figure: even her ribs are visible through her
emaciated and bony flesh. His use of varied materials and
textures also reflects his adherence to the principles of the
'New Sculpture'.

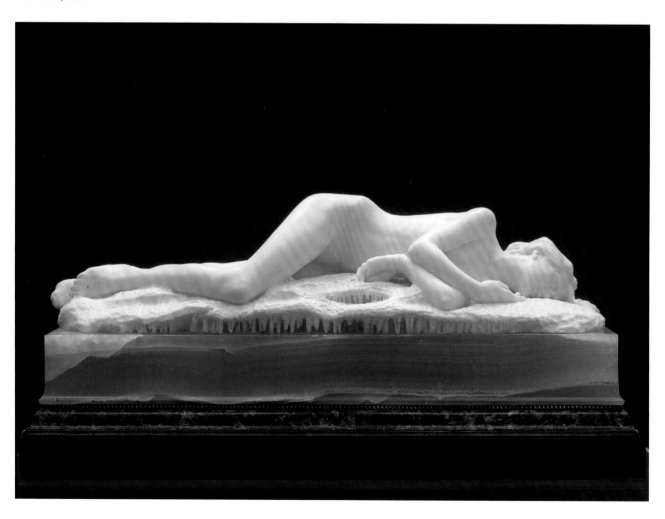

The Shortening Winter's Day is near a Close, 1903

Joseph Farquharson (1846-1935)

British

Oil on canvas, 117 x 171 cm

Purchased from the artist by Lever through Agnew and Son, 1903; inv. no. LL 3152

The artist became well-known in his lifetime for his investigations of light and colour. The challenging subject of white sheep against snow was one of his most popular themes. One contemporary review described this particular work as a *'tour de force'* of landscape painting because of its ingenuity in conveying sunlight and shadows.

On his holidays, Norway, 1901-2

John Singer Sargent (1856-1925)

American

Oil on canvas, 137 x 244 cm

Purchased by Lever, 1923; inv. no. LL 3136
(WHL 4730)

Alexander McCulloch, then a schoolboy at Winchester College, is resting after salmon fishing in Norway. The summer holidays were a bad time for salmon fishing in Britain and, with better communications, Norway became more fashionable at the end of the 19th century. Alexander was the son of the great collector, George McCulloch, from whose sale Lever bought many of the late Victorian masterpieces in the Main Hall. Sargent is best known for his dazzling society portraits of the 1880s and 1890s, and the descriptive power of his rapid, vigorous brush strokes is very evident here. After 1900 he gradually abandoned formal portraiture in favour of landscape, and the boy's casual but thoughtful pose within a carefully worked out natural setting very much reflects the artist's new and rather wider intentions.

'Jeunesse Dorée, 1934

Gerard Leslie Brockhurst (1890 - 1978)

British

Oil on board, 76.2 x 63.1 cm

Purchased by the Gallery, 1934; inv.no. LL 3908

The model for Jeunesse Dorée (and for much of the artist's work in the 1930s) was Kathleen (or Dorette) Woodward whom the artist met at the Royal Academy where she was a model for the students. They married in 1947. Brockhurst painted her under various fanciful titles, often combining as here a Renaissance format, Symbolist colours and intensity, an enticing sensuality with - from the title - a hint of upper class decadence more commonly associated with the 1920s than the 1930s.

At the 1934 Royal Academy the critics were most impressed by Brockhurst's hard finish and detail, but H Granville Fell observed that 'Mr Gerald Brockhurst continues to astonish us with his meticulous and sometimes disconcerting analysis of the opposite sex' and described 'Jeunesse Dorée' as 'sophisticated and worldy wise'.

Salem, 1908
Sydney Curnow Vosper (1866-1942)
British
Watercolour on paper, 71 x 73.5 cm
Purchased from the artist, 1909; inv. no LL 3446

Vosper painted this image in 1908 while visiting Llanbedr, North Wales possibly on a cycle trip. It shows the interior of the Baptist chapel Salem Cefncymerau built in 1850. Vosper paid local people sixpence an hour to model for the scene. The women all wear traditional Welsh dress with the distinctive steeple hats. Lever used the image as a promotional print for Sunlight Soap, much to the surprise of the artist. The picture's popularity is partly down to the wide circulation of this reproduction print, but it is also due to the way the work symbolises Welsh culture and identity.

The Decameron, 1915-16
John William Waterhouse (1849-1917)
British
Oil on canvas, 101 x 159 cm
Purchased by Lever from the artist, 1916; inv. no. LL 3133 (WHL 2754)

Boccaccio's *Decameron* of about 1353 relates the often rather picturesque and risqué stories told to each other by a group of young men and women who had taken refuge in the countryside from the plague in Florence. Suppressed sexual tension and emotion in the contrasted faces and very varied attitudes of the women is given added poignancy by the idyllic garden setting. The lutes, too, signify love and the artist has achieved great dramatic intensity from his static and motionless composition.

The Penitent Thief, 1918
Francis Derwent Wood (1872-1926)
British
Bronze, 35.5 x 28 x 23.5 cm
Presented to the Gallery by the sculptor's widow, 1945; inv. no. LL 729 (LS 13)

The poetic realism for which the sculptors of the 'New Sculpture' became famous in the last years of the 19th century became weakened under a deluge of commissions for rather conventional busts and monuments. Religious subject matter, so rich in opportunities for expression and meaning, was rare. This head, showing one of the two thieves crucified alongside Christ, is therefore of particular interest as it demonstrates so powerfully the sculptor's ability to manipulate and model surfaces with deep furrows and high, sharp ridges in order to produce a face of enormous power and poignancy.

The Friesian Bull, 1920-21
Alfred Jones Munnings (1878-1959)
British
Oil on canvas, 95.3 x 129 cm
Purchased from the artist by the Trustees of the Lady Lever Art Gallery, 1947; inv. no. LL 3915 (LP 69)

Munnings was both the most distinguished British animal painter of the 20th century and very interested in farming and country life. Naturally, therefore, he was fascinated by the new and immensely expensive black and white Friesian bulls which were changing the face of English dairy farming in the early 20th century. Here he contrasts the enormous bulk and power of the animal with its apparent placidity as it is led out by the herdsman. He actually witnessed the scene on the Devonshire farm of friends and found it pictorially irresistible. The free and rapid technique reflects his early style; his later work is more finished and detailed.

CHARITAS   SPES

Furniture

The Gallery's holdings of furniture range in date from the late 16th century to the beginning of the 19th, embracing what in Lever's lifetime was considered to be the definitive period of fine English cabinet-making. Lever was one of the earliest collectors to attempt to form a comprehensive collection of English furniture across this period, illustrating the particular features of successive styles, and the Lady Lever furniture collection constitutes one of his greatest achievements in the campaign to demonstrate the merits of British art. There is a certain irony in this, for Lever's instinctive liking for virtuosity and colour was much more in keeping with Continental taste, and led him to pursue the very grandest English furniture, which for much of the period in question was powerfully influenced by Continental, primarily French, styles. This is especially true of the outstanding group of marquetry and painted commodes (a type of low cabinet or chest of drawers, see pp. 62-66) of the 1760s-80s, by far Lever's favourite period within the long span covered by his collections.

In some cases, Lever's taste drew him to objects that have since been shown to have originated on the Continent, such as the French 17th-century cabinet-on-stand (p. 54) - though this is of a type made all over Europe, Britain included - and the remarkable 18th-century beadwork urn, once thought to be English but now believed to have been made in Brunswick, Germany (p. 66). But in at least one context Lever deliberately acquired French furniture: when an object was known or supposed to have had some connection with his political hero, Napoleon. The original 'Napoleon Room' in the Lady Lever Art Gallery (fig. 8), was filled with furniture and other objects that Lever had acquired for their associations with the Emperor, including the Fesch suite (see p. 72) and Orchardson's sitter's chair.

The Napoleon Room is one of five 'period rooms' in the Gallery, and distinct from the others in being not only devoted to a French style, but concerned with a personal cult. The other four are primarily intended to provide an appropriate setting for the furniture displayed in them: a decorative device that Lever also adopted in his houses, though then usually with new panelling made in the style of earlier periods. Between 1917 and 1919, Lever purchased genuine panelling for three of the rooms in the Gallery. The 'Tudor and Stuart Room' from Lambourne Hall in Essex (fig. 9), and the 'William and Mary Room', said to be from Walterclough Hall near Halifax, were both bought from Litchfield & Co, while the 'Early 18th-Century Room', from a house near Chatham, Kent, came from Arthur Edwards; but in all three cases the panelling had to be adapted and extended to fit the appointed spaces. The 'Adam Room', however, is an entirely new creation, apart from the 18th-century chimney-piece. It was designed for the Gallery by the furniture historian and stage designer Percy Macquoid, and executed by the firm of White Allom in 1924-5; the plasterwork is based on early Adam interiors of the 1760s, but arranged so

Fig. 8   The Napoleon Room, about 1922. In the 1960s this space was divided into two rooms.

densely as to make the room unmistakably Edwardian, and so in some respects the most successful of all the period rooms.

While the period rooms provided a quasi-historical context for Lever's presentation of successive developments in English furniture, it is the furniture shown outside these rooms, almost all of it 18th-century, that reveals his main personal preferences. Next to the 'Adam' and other neo-classical furniture, perhaps the greatest strength of the collection is the peculiarly English Palladian style furniture that evolved under the influence of William Kent in the 1720s-40s, of which Lever was a pioneer collector. At its most architectural, and Kentian, this style can be seen in the work of William Hallett - the mahogany cabinet from Kirtlington Park and the chairs from Longford Hall (see pp. 58-59) - and in the anonymous gilt and painted side tables from Stowe (see p. 57). Aspects of the style, such as the lion's masks and the shell motif, were also absorbed into the more domestic furniture of the period, as seen in the suite of walnut chairs by Thomas Moore (see p. 56).

William Hallett was one of the most distinguished cabinet-makers of his generation, whose influence touched the careers of several younger men in the same trade. John Cobb, who in the 1770s gained a high reputation for his marquetry (see p. 64), was for some

years in partnership with Hallett's former journeyman William Vile, and Vile & Cobb between them enjoyed a brief but highly productive period (1761-4) in service to the Royal Household. Hallett also promoted the career of his own nephew Samuel Norman by introducing him to James Whittle as a suitable son-in-law and partner.

Another major London cabinet-making dynasty was that of William and John Linnell, father and son, initially established by William as a carving workshop in the 1720s, and carried on by John until two or three years before his death in 1796. One of their most celebrated joint commissions was the 'Chinese' bedroom suite at Badminton, supplied in the early 1750s, to which belongs a pair of japanned china stands now in the Gallery (see p. 61). In the 1740s William Linnell had taken the imaginative step of sending his son to study at Hogarth's St. Martin's Lane Academy, and by the late 1760s John, now in charge of the firm, was producing sophisticated marquetry designs, drawn with a fluency that owes much to this unusual training (see p. 62). The style shows strong French influence, doubtless filtered through the Swedish cabinet-makers Georg Haupt and Christopher Fuhrlohg whom Linnell employed briefly when they first arrived in London in 1767 or '68, having just completed their training in Paris. While Haupt was soon summoned back to Sweden to become the King's cabinet-maker, Fuhrlohg remained in London and set up in business on his own account, producing furniture that, while unmistakably English, is of very pronounced French character (see p. 63).

Thomas Chippendale, now the most famous name in the history of English furniture, lacked the dynastic advantages enjoyed by several of his rivals. Born and trained in Yorkshire, he arrived in London without connections in the late 1740s, and the publication in 1754 of *The Gentleman and Cabinet-maker's Director,* on which his posthumous reputation largely rests, was an astute attempt to compensate for these deficiencies and make a very public bid for patronage. By 1762, when he published a third edition, he was in a position to boast that some of the designs had already been executed and had given 'entire satisfaction' (see p. 61). But by this date he was already moving away from the rococo style that dominates the *Director,* towards the new classicism promoted by Robert Adam.

The long-lived partnership of John Mayhew and William Ince (1758/9-1804), whose work is particularly well-represented in the Lady Lever collection (pp. 64-65), was also one of the most ambitious and innovative of their generation. Although only newly established in business, they responded directly to the publication of the *Director* with a rival work, published in 1762, *The Universal System of Household Furniture.* Like the *Director,* it featured designs almost entirely in the rococo style, and like Chippendale, Mayhew and Ince were already experimenting with the 'antique' taste within a few years of its appearance. On several commissions they worked closely with leading architects, especially Robert Adam in the 1760s-80s, and later Henry Holland.

Like Chippendale, George Brookshaw arrived in London from the provinces. A tradesman of a later generation, the so-called 'peintre-ébéniste' ('painter-cabinet-maker') was unusual for focusing almost entirely on painted furniture (see p. 70). He regularly advertised his specialist output in the London newspapers, and on at least one occasion attracted the custom of the Prince of Wales. But after 20 years' activity, he appears to have gone out of business in the mid-1790s, and temporarily assumed a false name (perhaps in order to conceal himself from creditors). When he resurfaced under his own name in 1804, it was as a teacher of flower-painting (a pursuit he had followed as a sideline while making furniture) and as the author and illustrator of an ambitious publication on fruit-growing, the *Pomona Britannica.*

Brookshaw's furniture was typically painted (and partly gilt) all over the surface, with no wood showing. But a slightly later fashion was for satinwood furniture with painted decoration on the wood, and the firm of Seddon, Sons & Shackleton is particularly known for this technique (see p. 71). Unlike Brookshaw, however, Seddons were an all-purpose firm operating on an enormous scale, and painted furniture was only one of their many branches of activity. Also unlike Brookshaw, the firm was exceptionally long-lived: founded by George Seddon in about 1753, it lasted, under various guises, until 1868.

Recent furniture studies have revealed the calibre of some furniture made outside London during the 18th century. The Lady Lever's extraordinary suite of 'Chinese' rococo chairs (see p. 60) is now known to have been made by a cabinetmaker operating in Berwick-upon-Tweed; by no means a major commercial centre. With hindsight, a provincial origin for this suite is entirely credible, for it is very much an aberration in terms of mainstream London furniture making, and it was doubtless its bizarre quality that largely appealed to Lever.

This suite also represents another significant strand in Lever's taste - his interest in the chinoiserie style in English furniture, ranging from the literal imitations of Oriental lacquer cabinets favoured in the late 17th century (see p. 55), to the more inventive creations of the rococo, such as the Badminton bedroom suite (see p. 61), the Chippendale dressing-table (see p. 61) and Lever's collection of chairs. The exceptionally rare painted leather chairs from Parham Park (see p. 55) reflect a halfway point between these two approaches, while the Anglo-Indian buffalo-horn chair (see p. 71) is a late 18th-century example of the same pursuit of the exotic. The remarkable collector's cabinet (see p. 73) is now thought to belong to an early 19th-century revival of the 'Chinese' rococo style. Such objects were completely in tune with Lever's taste for the strange and rare, a taste that he also satisfied in many other areas of his collection. It is pieces of this nature, in some cases unique, in others simply the most outstanding examples of their kind, that make Lever's furniture collection not only highly personal, but also, judged by the most exacting and objective standards, one of the most distinguished collections ever to have been assembled.

Fig. 9   The Tudor and Stuart Room, about 1922, with the state bed from Dyrham Park (where it has been returned on loan). The overmantel on the left is inlaid with the initials and date, 'TB' (supposedly for Thomas Barfoot), 1571, but these are now thought to be 19th-century additions; the panelling dates mainly from the early 17th century.

Nonsuch chest, 1592; the stand, about 1900

German or English

Oak inlaid with rosewood, maple, box(?) and green-stained holly or sycamore, with wrought iron handles and hinges, on ash stand, chest 56 x 122.5 x 57.5 cm (height with stand 100 cm)

Presented to the Gallery by Mrs Percy Macquoid, 1927; inv. no. LL 4723 (L 6)

Chests of this type acquired the name 'Nonsuch' from the mistaken belief that they portray Henry VIII's famous palace at Cheam. The buildings depicted are actually in a conventional 'antique' style found on 16th-century furniture from southern Germany, especially Cologne. However, this chest could also have been made in London by one of the German community settled in Southwark (outside the jurisdiction of the London guilds). Its history is unknown before 1890 when the furniture historian Percy Macquoid bought it at the sale of William Maskell of Bude Haven, Cornwall. The stand was made later, apparently by Macquoid himself. Theresa Macquoid presented the chest and stand to commemorate her husband's association with the Gallery, for which at Lever's request he designed the Adam Room and wrote the original catalogue of the furniture collection.

Cabinet-on-stand, about 1680

French

Olive veneer with marquetry of ebony, ivory, green-stained bone, box, sabicu and other woods, ebonised beech(?) feet and mouldings, gilt wood carving and brass mounts, on a pine carcase, with walnut, pine and oak drawers, 188.5 x 135 x 51 cm

Purchased by Lever in 1918; inv. no. LL 4237 (X 266)

The cabinet was the most prestigious type of furniture in the 17th century, apart from the state bed, and gave rise to the English term 'cabinet-maker' for the most skilled of the wood-working trades. Similar examples to this were made throughout northern Europe, often with a matching suite comprising a pier table, mirror and candlestands. This piece appears to be inspired by the outstanding, jewel-like cabinets from the workshop of Pierre Gole, cabinet-maker to the French Court. The back of one of the small drawers is inscribed 'Baudory', perhaps the name of a previous owner.

Cabinet-on-stand, about 1690; the stand, about 1680

The cabinet Dutch (?), the stand English

Japanned pine and oak with brass mounts, and silvered pine stand, cabinet 87.5 x 89 x 51.5 cm, stand 79.5 x 114 x 57 cm, overall height 165 cm

Cabinet purchased by Lever in 1918; inv. no. LL 4474 (X 2648)

Stand of unknown provenance; inv. no. LL 4475

The craze in the late 17th century for all things oriental - porcelain, silks and lacquer especially - created a demand that could not be met by the imports of the Dutch and English East India Companies, and the gap was filled by European imitations, which were not necessarily considered inferior. This cabinet in imitation lacquer, generally known as japanning, is a direct translation of a Japanese form, with its distinctive bracket base. The silvered stand, inspired by Louis XIV's solid silver furniture at Versailles, is roughly contemporary but not the original one for this cabinet.

Chair, about 1705-10

English

Beech and walnut, upholstered in gilt and painted leather, close-nailed, 101.5 x 51.8 x 56.3 cm

Purchased by Lever in 1920; inv. no. LL 4102 (X 4070)

One of a set of seven chairs from Parham Park, Sussex, which retain their original upholstery and gilt leather covers, an exceptionally rare survival. The Chinese theme of the painted decoration is also carried through to the seat frames: such features as the 'ears' near the feet are inspired by Chinese furniture of the sort made for the home market, very little of which was exported to Europe at this period. The shape of the back resembles a celebrated set of needlework-covered chairs at Canons Ashby, Northamptonshire, supplied in 1714 by the Royal upholsterer Thomas Phill. Phill also delivered an armchair (now lost) covered in 'black Spanish Leather' with a nailed border, which sounds comparable to the Parham chairs.

Settee, about 1723; the tapestry, about 1610

English

Walnut (veneered and solid) with marquetry of holly and apple (?), oak rails, wool and silk tapestry covers, 113.7 x 122.5 x 75.9 cm

Purchased by Lever in 1920; inv. no. LL 4234 (X 3846)

The arms painted on the cresting are those of Thomas Wyndham of Hawkchurch, Dorset, and Elizabeth Helyar of Yately, Hampshire, who were married in about 1723. The settee, doubtless made to commemorate the marriage, is possibly of provincial manufacture; the initials 'CF', perhaps those of the maker, are branded on the oak seat frame. The curiously high back and deep seat suggest the settee was specially made to frame the Sheldon tapestry cushion covers, depicting the virtues of Faith, Charity, Hope, Justice and Temperance, which were then over 100 years old: an unusual antiquarian gesture at that period.

Chair, 1734

Thomas Moore (d. 1738)

English

Walnut, beech and oak, later cover of voided cotton-velvet, 98.6 x 63.5 x 62 cm

Acquired by Lever in 1903 or 1904; inv. no. LL 4127 (H 495)

One of a suite of eight (but originally ten) chairs supplied to Sir Dudley Ryder in 1734 by Thomas Moore, formerly the partner of Daniel Bell (the partnership appears to have been dissolved in the same year, when Bell was appointed cabinet-maker and chair-maker to the Royal Household). The chairs were described on Moore's bill as 'ten hansome Wallnuttree Chairs broad banister backs cutt in a shape with scrole tops finneard [veneered] with very good wood, loose compass seats... with rich carved fore feet with Lyons faces on Ye Knees and Lyons Paws & O. Ge [ogee] back feet with scroles and carved shells to ye fore rails'. The bill also records another similar suite of walnut chairs and a pair of gilt wood pier tables and mirrors en suite. No charge is noted for travelling expenses, so this furniture may have been delivered to a London house.

Side-table, about 1740

English

Gilt and painted pine, the top veneered in calcite 'onyx', with solid white marble borders, 88 x 189.5 x 97 cm

Purchased by Lever in 1919; inv. no. LL 4232 (X 3743)

Decorated with masks of Diana (a crescent moon in her hair) and satyrs, this table and its pair were at Stowe House, Buckinghamshire until the great sale of 1848 when they were bought by Sir Philip Pauncefort-Duncombe for Great Brickhill Manor nearby. A generation earlier than the Stowe state bed (see p. 60), they are in the Palladian style associated with William Kent, who was employed at Stowe by Lord Cobham in the 1730s. The tops are probably early 19th-century replacements, that is, 18th-century veneered slabs, extended by new borders fixed with big brass studs.

Armchair, about 1740

Scottish (?)

Gilt pine and beech, covers of linen canvas embroidered in wool and silk in tent-stitch, 108 x 81.3 x 67.4 cm

Purchased by Lever in 1918; inv. no. LL 4205 (X 2973)

The embroidery on the back depicts the *Sacrifice of Iphigenia,* the post-Homeric story that Agamemnon's daughter was sacrificed to appease the goddess Artemis, who had induced a calm to prevent the Greek fleet sailing to Troy. Here Agamemnon and Achilles look on as, at the last minute, Artemis takes pity and spirits Iphigenia away. The seat is embroidered more simply with a dog chasing a fox. These covers are original and the borders show that they were specially designed for this chair. It is one of an original set of at least six, and several other examples with very similar embroidery are known, mostly from houses in Scotland.

Settee, about 1760

English

Gilt beech, covers of linen canvas embroidered in wool and silk in tent stitch and cross-stitch, decorative brass nails, and red moreen on the back, 102.5 x 223.2 x 88.4 cm

Purchased by Lever in 1919; inv. no. LL 4226 (X 3350)

The covers, which may be original, depict pastoral scenes and vases of flowers in cartouches. The scene at the left end of the back is adapted from an engraving, *Le Soir,* one of the series *Les Pastorales,* engraved by Claudine Stella after designs by her uncle Jacques Stella, and published in Paris in 1664. Such subjects strongly appealed to rococo taste a century later.

Chair, about 1737-40

Attributed to William Hallett (about 1707-81)

English

Virginia walnut, solid and veneered, and partly gilt; beech seat rails; original drop-in caned seat beneath the later fixed upholstery and wool-velvet cover, 96 x 59.6 x 62 cm

Purchased by Lever in 1917; inv. no. LL 4064 (X 2020)

One of a set of five chairs which almost certainly originated at Holkham Hall, Norfolk, seat of the Cokes, Earls of Leicester. They were sold from another Coke family house, Longford Hall, Derbyshire, in 1917. The model is inspired by the designs of William Kent, the architect of Holkham and creator of the Palladian style in interior decoration. Two variant chairs remain at Holkham, the finer one probably a 'pattern chair' (p. 60) that William Hallett made for Lord Leicester's approval in 1738. The other was probably ordered locally, in an attempt to procure the set more cheaply, but the final commission was evidently given to Hallett after all. The chairs have drop-in caned seats beneath the later upholstery, an unusual feature also found in another set of Kentian chairs at Holkham.

Cabinet-on-chest, about 1747

Attributed to William Hallett (about 1707-81)

English

Sabicu (?) and purplewood veneer with brass inlay and mounts and mahogany carvings, partly gilt, on a carcase of mahogany (the upper section) and pine (lower section), with drawers of mahogany (upper section) and oak (lower section), 249 x 150 x 54 cm

Purchased by Lever in 1911; inv. no. LL 4416 (HR 188)

This stylish Palladian cabinet comes from Kirtlington Park, Oxfordshire, which was built about 1742-6 by Sir James Dashwood. It was probably made by William Hallett, the principal cabinet-maker employed by Sir James in furnishing the house, who was paid £425 in 1747 and further smaller sums up to 1752. The striking male terms supporting the base section suggest that it was intended for a room with a very specific, and imposing, decorative programme. The carcase has latterly been raised by about two inches between these figures.

State bed, 1757-9

Designed by Giovanni Battista Borra (1712-86)

English

Gilt mahogany and pine (the gilding renewed), silk taffeta, gilt and red rope; embroidery of gold, red and blue metal foil, gold and silver metal thread, silver and steel spangles, silk on card or vellum, coloured paste jewels and beads, with silk-velvet, pearls and metal thread fringe; modern red silk shantung and yellow watered silk hangings with wool and silk galloon and fringe, 447.5 x 297.5 x 272 cm approx.

Purchased by Lever at the Stowe House sale in 1921; inv. no. LL 4207 (X 4091)

Designed by the Piedmontese architect GB Borra for the State Bedroom at Stowe House, Buckinghamshire. It was originally hung with Genoese crimson damask. The coat of arms and cypher, in the headboard and canopy respectively, are late 18th-century work but were introduced to the bed when it was refurbished for Queen Victoria's visit to Stowe in 1845. The remaining hangings reflect the scheme adopted at that time, but all except the crimson silk in the canopy are modern replacements.

Chairs, about 1766

William Davidson (about 1729-73)

English (Berwick-upon-Tweed)

Mahogany, beech and pine, modern silk damask covers, 105.8 x 67.9 x 72.3 cm; 105.3 x 67.2 x 70 cm

Purchased by Lever in 1915; inv. nos. LL 4068 (X 419), LL 4072 (X 416)

Two remarkable chinoiserie chairs from a set of seven (and a much altered sofa), made for Sir John (later Lord) Delaval at Ford Castle, Northumberland. William Davidson was evidently referring to this suite when he wrote from Berwick to Lady Delaval at Ford, in 1766: 'your 6 Chenise Chairs & fly table shall be sett about and forwarded in dew time. To your desire have sent you a Pattron Chair... it is wanting 2 Brass Buttons behind'. The chair on the left is the pattern chair, with different options for the treatment of the seat rails: the other chair shows further modifications that were adopted for the rest of the suite. The loose backs are indeed held in place by two swivelling brass 'buttons' in the form of Chinese masks.

China stand, 1752-4
William Linnell (about 1703-63) and John Linnell (1729-96)

English

Japanned pine and mahogany; 149 x 50.6 x 26 cm

Purchased by Lever in 1922; inv. no. LL 45 (X 4150)

One of a pair which comes from a celebrated suite of furniture made by the Linnells for the 'Chinese' state bedchamber at Badminton House, Gloucestershire. The state bed is now in the Victoria & Albert Museum, together with the commode and two of the eight armchairs. A drawing by John Linnell (William's son) for the chairs suggests that he probably designed the entire suite, although the workshop was still run by his father at this date. The drawing shows a different colour scheme in red, blue and yellow, traces of which have been found on some of the other pieces in the suite. The present scheme probably dates from the mid- or late 19th century.

Dressing-table, about 1760
Thomas Chippendale (1718-79)

English

Rosewood (veneered and solid) and simulated rosewood graining, carved oil-gilt mahogany and water-gilt lime(?), brass and ormolu mounts and ivory handles, on a pine, walnut, mahogany, oak and lime(?) carcase, 206.2 x 128.5 x 62.5 cm

Purchased by Lever in 1916; inv. no. LL 4245 (X 1608)

'Chinese' variation on a rococo design published by Chippendale in the 3rd edition (1762) of *The Gentleman and Cabinet-Maker's Director* (plate LII), and probably one of those that he referred to in commenting on this plate:

'Two Dressing-Tables have been made of Rose-Wood, from this Design, which gave an entire Satisfaction: All the Ornaments were gilt.' It was probably made for Lady Arniston, who was a client of Chippendale's and whose descendants sold it in 1916. Notable features of this piece include the hinged brass brackets on which the mirror moves backwards and forwards, and the carved wood - not metal - open fretwork of the upper cupboard doors.

Commode, about 1768-70
John Linnell (1729-96)

English

Marquetry of maple, purplewood, rosewood, walnut, mahogany, holly, fruitwoods, sycamore and other woods, with ormolu mounts, on a pine, mahogany and oak carcase, 86 x 107 x 46 cm

Purchased by Lever in 1919; inv. no. LL 49 (X 3110)

This is related to furniture supplied by John Linnell to Osterley Park, Middlesex, in the late 1760s, as well as to some designs for commodes among a large group of Linnell's drawings (now in the Victoria & Albert Museum), which show him to have been an accomplished draughtsman. This skill is reflected in the drawing of the marquetry cartouches and trophies on this piece. This decoration perhaps also reveals the influence of the Paris-trained Swedish cabinet-makers, Georg Haupt and Christopher Fuhrlohg, who were briefly employed in his workshop at about this time. The subjects of the trophies, Music and Painting, suggest the commode was intended for a drawing room devoted to the arts.

Commode, about 1770

English

Gilt and painted mahogany and painted in mahogany and pine, with ormolu and lacquered brass mounts, 88.5 x 143.5 x 72.5 cm

Acquired by Lever in 1903 or 1904; inv. no. LL 4376 (H 150)

This commode, from Seaton Delaval Hall, Northumberland, was originally fitted inside with '13 Copper front[ed] Drawers inlaid in mother of Pearl', and had a pair of corner cupboards *en suite*. The suite was sold to Sir John Delaval in 1776 by John Cobb, on commission from its owner John Carrack, a haberdasher and hosier, who seems to have been speculating in furniture (this suite had by then been on his hands for several years). The maker remains unidentified, but the bombé shape (curved in two planes at once), the construction and the decorative treatment all indicate an immigrant craftsman.

Commode, about 1772

Christopher Fuhrlohg (active 1762-87)

English

Marquetry of harewood, tulipwood, purplewood, sycamore, fruitwoods, holly, walnut, mahogany, box, ebony and other woods, with ormolu and brass mounts, on an oak carcase with mahogany drawers; 99.5 x 142.5 x 45.5 cm

Acquired by Lever in 1903 or 1904; inv. no. LL 4233 (H 286)

The breakfront form and the trellis parquetry reflect Fuhrlohg's recent training in Paris , but the medallion of Diana is in the distinctive style of Angelica Kauffman, who worked in London in the 1760s-70s. Indeed the medallion on a companion commode is signed in Latin, 'C. Fuhrlohg, 1772, after Angelica Kauffman'. Fuhrlohg could have been following original drawings by Kauffman, for no engraved source for either composition is known. The doors have been converted from sliding panels which originally ran on tracks under the case. The marquetry in the frieze is also a later introduction.

Commode, 1775-80

Thomas Chippendale (1718-79)

English

Marquetry of East Indian satinwood, tulipwood, purplewood, fruitwoods, rosewood, sycamore, harewood and box, with ormolu and lacquered brass mounts, on a pine and rosewood carcase, with mahogany and oak drawers, 91 x 147.5 x 62.5 cm

Purchased by Lever in 1914; inv. no. LL 4247 (X 19)

This commode has such strong stylistic affinities with the neo-classical furniture supplied by Thomas Chippendale to Harewood House in the 1770s, that his authorship of this piece is beyond doubt. But it is not known for whom, or for what house, it was originally made. It was allegedly given away by the Duke of Wellington to his campaign chaplain, probably in the 1820s or 30s, and the pair to it, now in a private collection, appears to have been acquired at about the same time by a Liverpool merchant and politician, Ashton Yates.

Commode, about 1770

John Cobb (about 1715-78)

English

Marquetry of mahogany, satinwood, rosewood, tulipwood, sycamore, walnut, box, holly, purplewood, fruitwoods and birch, with brass mounts on a mahogany and pine carcase, 92.5 x 115 x 60cm

Purchased by Lever in 1920; inv no LL56 (X3733)

The top shows the coat of arms (with a baron's coronet) of the commode's first owner Lord Hyde, later created Earl of Clarendon. Cobb's most celebrated work is a slightly larger marquetry commode of very similar design and construction to this one, which he supplied to Paul Methuen at Corsham Court, Wiltshire in 1772, with a pair of candlestands.

Commode, about 1773

John Mayhew (1736-1811) & William Ince (d. 1804)

English

Marquetry of birch, satinwood, tulipwood, kingwood, holly, avodire(?), fruitwoods, purplewood, walnut, ebony, box and sycamore, with ormolu and lacquered brass mounts, on a mahogany and pine carcase, 90.5 x 132 x 64.5 cm

Purchased by Lever at the Earl of Home's sale in 1919; inv. no. LL 57 (X 3398)

This handsome commode was supplied to Archibald Douglas (later Lord Douglas) for his London house in Pall Mall, which he was also filling with French furniture in the early 1770s (much of it smuggled in under diplomatic cover). Following French practice, the commode came with a pair of corner cupboards (which are now in an American collection). The simple box-like form, contrasting with the very elaborate decoration, was pioneered by Mayhew and Ince in the 1760s. It must have seemed startlingly austere at a time when English commodes were, almost by definition, serpentine.

Commode, about 1775-80

John Mayhew (1736-1811) & William Ince (d. 1804)

English

Marquetry of harewood, ebony, holly, East Indian and West Indian satinwood, purplewood, hornbeam(?), rosewood, tulipwood, box and mahogany, with painted copper medallion and ormolu and lacquered brass mounts, on a mahogany and pine carcase, 90.5 x 138 x 56 cm

Purchased by Lever at the Bretby Heirlooms sale in 1918; inv. no. LL 4225 (X 2661)

In 1774 Robert Adam designed the first so-called 'Etruscan' interior: the Countess of Derby's dressing-room at Derby House in London, inspired by the decoration of Greek vases (which were then thought to be Etruscan, see p. 109). The commode for the room was manufactured by Mayhew and Ince, who subsequently adapted the model (with or without Adam's consent) for other clients. This version, centring a painted copper medallion of Cupid and the Three Graces, belonged to the Earls of Chesterfield, and was probably ordered by the 5th Earl for Chesterfield House in Mayfair.

Commode, about 1780

John Mayhew (1736-1811) & William Ince (d. 1804)

English

Marquetry of makore(?), kingwood, tulipwood, purplewood, sycamore, box, ivory, ebony, holly, fruitwoods and other woods, with ormolu mounts, on a mahogany and pine carcase, 84.5 x 144.5 x 61 cm

Acquired by Lever between 1901 and 1903; inv. no. LL 4246 (H 526)

In this remarkable design, the bold serpentine shape of the top is echoed by the profile of the aprons in the opposite plane. The charging bull, derived from an antique gem, suggests this was part of a major iconographic scheme, and the apparently unique ormolu mounts also point to the high status of this still unidentified commission. A related (but less sophisticated) pair of commodes at Broadlands, Hampshire, was probably among the furniture supplied by Mayhew and Ince to Viscount Palmerston.

Urn-on-stand, about 1760

German (Brunswick)

Glass beads, enamel plaques, shells, mother-of-pearl, agate, wool embroidery and gilt metal mounts, on a pine core, with later gilt wood finial, 170.5 x 50 x 49.2 cm

Purchased by Lever in 1919; inv. no. LL 4267 (X 3686-7)

This was probably made in the specialist workshop established in Brunswick by an apparently Dutch immigrant, Johann Michael van Selow, active from 1755 to 1767. However, most of the production was flat panels for table-tops and few three-dimensional pieces like this are known. Stylistically this is still a baroque object, an indication of the provincial character of North German taste at a time when, elsewhere in Europe, the rococo was at its height. The only trace of the rococo to be found here is in the coarse gilt metal mounts under the 'cover' of the urn and at the base.

Commode, about 1765-70

English

Oak, partly gilt, the top veneered in red breccia marble, 91.5 x 141.5 x 72 cm

Purchased by Lever in 1918; inv. no. LL 4321 (X 2922)

The use of solid oak as a show wood on an object of such grandeur is seemingly unparalleled in English 18th-century furniture. It was presumably used at the request of the patron, and may have come from a tree with particular associations. The carved and gilt angles and feet are copied from contemporary gilt metal mounts. This commode may be from the same unidentified workshop as a group of lacquer and japanned commodes that feature these mounts, but one of which has the same patterns in gilt wood, as here.

Globe clock, about 1765-70

Jean Romilly (1714-96)

French

Bronze, ormolu and enamel, 113.3 x 71.5 x 63.6 cm

Purchased by Lever at the Stafford House sale, 1913;
inv. no. LL 4464 (HH 241)

The time is marked by the central band revolving past the serpent's
tongue. Three putti share the burden of the Earth, traditionally
borne by Atlas. Their attributes represent the four elements:
Earth (the rock they stand on), Fire (coming out of the rock), Water
(spilling from the ewer) and Air (in their billowing draperies).

The clock may have been designed by the leading marchand-
mercier (a sort of dealer-cum-decorator) Simon Philippe Poirier, for
whom Romilly sometimes worked. Its early history is unknown, but
by 1839 it was at Stafford House, the opulent town house of the
Duke of Sutherland: it stood on its present pedestal in the ground-
floor Drawing Room, in the centre of a circular ottoman upholstered
in 'Purple and Amber Satin, with a deep silk fringe'.

Lever bought a number of works of art at the Stafford House sale
in 1913; he also purchased the house itself, which he renamed
Lancaster House and presented to the nation to become the first
home of the Museum of London.

Dressing-table, about 1770-90

French

Straw marquetry on a poplar(?) carcase, 74.6 x 91.5 x 45.5 cm

Purchased by Lever in 1910; inv. no. LL 4619 (H 218)

As with the filigree paper cabinet (p. 69), this is an unusually large example of such a delicate material to survive intact. It is the most ambitious instance of the straw-work technique in the Gallery's collection of some hundred pieces. The pastoral scenes are doubtless derived from engravings, like the embroidered scenes on the rococo settee (p. 58). The table is said to have belonged to one of George III's equerries, who could have acquired it in Paris.

Cabinet-on-stand, about 1780-90

English

Filigree paper, mezzotints and beads,
stained holly or sycamore and ebonised
pear, and brass handles, on a pine carcase,
146.5 x 61.5 x 45 cm

Purchased by Lever in 1919;
inv. no. LL 4224 (X 3733)

Filigree paperwork was a fashionable
ladies' accomplishment in the 18th and
early 19th centuries. In 1786 *The New
Ladies' Magazine* published patterns
'suitable for tea-caddies, toilets, chimneypieces, screens, cabinets, frames, picture
ornament etc'. Few pieces of full-scale
furniture in this fragile medium now
survive. This cabinet was sold by the
descendants of the merchant John
Julius Angerstein (1735-1823), whose
picture collection forms the nucleus of
the National Gallery. It could have been
decorated by either of his two wives, or it
may be a professional production.

Settee, about 1785

Attributed to George Brookshaw (1751-1823)

English

Gilt and painted beech(?), covers decorated with knotting in silk, re-applied to new silk ground, 100.6 x 215 x 79.7 cm

Acquired by Lever before 1907; inv. no. LL 4160 (H 259)

Part of a suite of two settees and six elbow chairs, formerly at Berechurch Hall, Essex, painted with scenes from literature and mythology and with delicate floral decoration in Brookshaw's characteristic style. The frames are now gilded all over, but originally the ribbons around the oval backs were picked out in blue. The embroidered seat-covers have been cut down from larger pieces (perhaps curtains), and were probably put on this suite in the early 19th century.

Secretaire commode, about 1785-90

George Brookshaw (1751-1823)

English

Painted mahogany and pine, gilt mahogany and composition mouldings, 97 x 187.5 x 62.5 cm

Purchased by Lever in 1914; inv. no. LL 4322 (X 20)

Originally from Birmingham, George Brookshaw set up a cabinet-making business in London in 1777. His workshop dealt almost exclusively in painted furniture, typically with closely observed floral decoration and figurative medallions adapted from engravings, chiefly after Angelica Kauffman. The medallions on the present commode (all derived from Kauffman) represent *Una and the Lion* (on top), and the lovers *Damon and Musidora* and *Paris and Oenone*. Brookshaw also operated as a teacher of flower-painting, and in the 1790s he abandoned his furniture practice in favour of publishing drawing-manuals, and a lavishly illustrated work on fruit-growing, the *Pomona Britannica*.

Elbow chair, about 1780-90

Anglo-Indian

Buffalo horn with gilt decoration, caned seat under later upholstery and figured satin cover, later painted and gilt iron (?) repair-straps, 90.4 x 57.1 x 54.3 cm

Purchased by Lever, 1919; inv. no. LL 4509 (X 3425)

This is similar in form to Anglo-Indian chairs made of ivory, but appears to be a unique surviving example of buffalo horn. It is said to have belonged to Warren Hastings, Governor General of India from 1774-84, and almost certainly formed part of a present from an Indian princess to his wife in 1784. Hastings informed his wife that the gift included two chairs of 'buffalo horn most delicately formed,...not designed for fat folks, nor romps; nor proper for you, my elegant Marion, to use in the presence of your husband'.

Writing-cabinet, about 1795-1800

Attributed to Seddon, Sons & Shackleton

English

Satinwood, purplewood, satin birch and other veneers, partly painted, on a mahogany carcase, 164.8 x 98.2 x 42 cm

Purchased by Lever in 1915; inv. no. LL 4154 (X 294)

The design of this cabinet is highly sophisticated in its three-dimensional play on sections of circles and ellipses. It is closely comparable to a mahogany writing-table in The Metropolitan Museum of Art, New York, bearing the trade label of Seddon, Sons & Shackleton. Thomas Sheraton also shows a related, but less complex, design in *The Cabinet-Maker and Upholsterer's Drawing-Book* (1793), for a cabinet 'to accommodate a lady with conveniences for writing, reading, and holding her trinkets'. By 1901 this piece was in the collection of the Liverpool shipper William Imrie, who also owned Burne-Jones' *The Tree of Forgiveness,* now in the Gallery's collection.

Writing-table, about 1785-90, repainted 1792

Painted by John Thomas Serres (1759-1825)

English

Painted mahogany and pine with brass mounts, 103.5 x 74 x 52.7 cm

Purchased by Lever in 1912; inv. no. LL 46 (H 437)

The seascapes, mostly of British ports, are signed and dated (1792) by JT Serres, Marine Painter to George III, who must have been commissioned to redecorate this writing-table within a very few years of its initial manufacture. To make his task easier, the table was sawn up into flat components that could be held on an easel, which were afterwards nailed together again, and this crude construction was disguised by the thick black borders. Like these borders, the trophies at the top of the legs are by a different hand, and below these the legs retain their original (pre to Serres) decoration. The table is in the form of a French *bonheur-du-jour,* with a fitted compartment on top, but its cupboard-doors were nailed shut when the table was re-assembled.

Armchair, about 1805-6

Designed by Dionisio Santi (b. 1786) and Lorenzo Santi (1783–1839)

Italian (Rome)

Gilt walnut and beech, silk embroidered covers with silk-covered gimp, 106.4 x 75.7 x 73 cm

Purchased by Lever in 1919; inv. no. LL 4640 (X 3621)

Typically Italian in its sculptural quality, this belongs to a large suite designed by the Santi brothers and made in Rome for Napoleon's uncle Cardinal Fesch, who served as the Emperor's ambassador to the Pope from 1803. In 1806 Napoleon suddenly recalled him, before the suite could be finished, and following the battle of Waterloo it was sold - still with no covers - from the Cardinal's house in Paris in 1816. The embroidered covers shown here were placed on the suite for the collector George Watson Taylor, around 1820. The chairs are now displayed with new silk covers to protect the originals underneath.

Armchair, about 1815-20

Attributed to Jean-Jacques Werner (1791–1849)

French

Gilt beech (the gilding renewed), later silk brocatelle covers, 109.1 x 68.6 x 66.1 cm

Purchased by Lever in 1913; inv. no. LL 4286 (HH 249)

Like the Fesch furniture, Lever bought this chair for its association with Napoleon, for it was alleged to have been at his palace of Malmaison until removed by the 1st Earl Cowley, who was British ambassador to Paris from 1852 to 1867. However, the chair is now thought to date from after the fall of Napoleon, and if it was indeed taken from Malmaison by Lord Cowley, it cannot have been part of the furnishings from Napoleon I's time, which were sold in 1829. The crown in the centre of the cresting is a later insertion.

Cabinet-on-stand, about 1820-30

English

Veneers of amboyna, padouk, pollard oak, walnut and numerous other exotic and native woods, rosewood and mahogany mouldings and ivory bells, on an oak and mahogany carcase; the stand rosewood and pine, 260.5 x 192.7 x 64 cm

Purchased by Lever from the Percy Dean sale in 1909; presented to the Gallery by the 3rd Viscount Leverhulme in 1980; inv. no. LL 4032 (H 159)

Though inspired by mid-18th-century models, such as Chippendale's designs for 'China Cases' in *The Gentleman and Cabinet-maker's Director,* this is now thought to belong to the early 19th-century rococo revival. It is a collector's cabinet, ultimately derived from 17th-century examples (see pp. 54-55), and probably intended for specimens of natural history - the different woods veneered on the drawers also forming a collection in themselves. It is said to have come from the family of the Earls of Guilford, and could possibly have been made for the Rev Charles Augustus North (1785-1825), grandson of the 1st Earl, whose collection of porcelain, bronzes and French furniture, as well as his 'valuable hot-house and green-house plants', were sold after his death.

Textiles

The Lady Lever Art Gallery's textiles collection is especially rich in examples of British embroidery, and in particular embroidered pictures of which it has over a hundred – one of the largest collections in the country. It also has fine items of 17th- and 18th-century costume, accessories and furnishings, including several tapestries from important series. But only about half of the embroidered pictures in Lever's possession at his death are now in the Gallery, the rest having been sold by his executors in 1925-6. (Another part of the collection, which decorated his Rivington bungalow, Roynton Cottage, was destroyed in 1913 in an arson attack by a suffragette.) The emphasis on embroidered pictures reflects collecting fashion at the beginning of the 20th century when Lever began buying embroideries. His interest was probably spurred by his furnishing of Hall-i'-th'-Wood, a house near his native town of Bolton, as a museum of 16th- and 17th-century domestic life. Almost all of this type of embroidery was worked by amateur young women and teenagers, either as part of their domestic education or to decorate their homes and fill their leisure hours. Lever was probably partly attracted to it because he saw it as proof of the high degree of decorative skill and technical craft that 'ordinary' British people could achieve.

The earliest examples of embroidery in the collection are a set of late 16th- or early 17th-century valances for a four-poster bed, embroidered with scenes illustrating the Old Testament story of Queen Athaliah and the boy king Joash (2 Kings verse 11 and 2 Chronicles verses 22-23). These had been turned into 'pictures' by framing and as such are typical of several 'pictures' in the collection, which were originally worked as furnishings to cover mirror frames, chair-backs, cushions and young women's work-caskets. Caskets were the culmination of a girl's domestic education and were often embroidered with Old Testament scenes considered most suitable by a parent or governess for a teenage girl: the love match between Isaac and Rebecca, or the intended sacrifice by Abraham of his son Isaac, one of the most commonly embroidered biblical scenes in 17th-century Britain, which could illustrate the Commandment of honouring your parents (see p. 79).

The Gallery has some fine examples of 17th-century mirror frames and caskets. Several show the distinctive style of raised work, popular in the second half of the 17th century, in which padded figures in very high relief, a well as gold and silver thread and lace, mica and seed pearls, were incorporated into embroidered pictures. The collecting of raised work was popularised from the beginning of the 20th century by art publications, which often referred to it as 'stumpwork'. A prime example of the style is *The Drowning of the Pharaoh in the Red Sea* (see p. 79). This picture is rare in having accompanying documentation which helped identify the embroiderer and provided illuminating information about her social, economic and religious context. The collection also includes several other elaborately worked pictures from the Stuart period. Unlike these pieces created by young amateurs, many of the 17th-century costume accessories particularly the elaborate gloves never intended for daily wear (see p. 81), were worked by professionals in workshops.

Not surprisingly, Lever was also attracted to 18th-century needlework which complemented his furniture collection. He acquired a number of pastoral scenes, most of which, as was common in the 18th century, were embroidered on fine linen canvas and intended either as furnishing textiles to cover screens, settees and chairs, or as pictures to decorate dressing-room walls and chimneypieces. More unusual among collectors of embroidered pictures was Lever's taste for late Georgian and Regency needleworks, which were partly embroidered, partly painted in watercolour onto silk (see p. 80). Usually hands and faces, the most difficult details to embroider satisfactorily, were painted, and the rest of the picture embroidered, providing a way by which ladies could display their accomplishments in what was considered an especially feminine art form. The speckled stitches frequently used on these painted silk pictures recreated the effect of the stipple engravings, sometimes of works by women artists such as Angelica Kauffmann (1741-1806), which often provided the basis for designs.

A growing number of these pictures have been identified as being based on theatrical and literary scenes.

Most of the small collection of tapestries was acquired between 1915 and 1920 and includes a number of important works. The Gobelins group came from Lews Castle, Stornoway, and Lever purchased them in 1918, at the same time as buying the castle itself with the Isle of Lewis. Lews Castle had been built in 1847 and lavishly furnished in a 'baronial' style by another Victorian entrepreneur businessman, Sir James Matheson (d. 1878), who had made his fortune partly through the Chinese opium trade and founded the Far Eastern business empire of Jardine Matheson. The Gobelins tapestries were extensively damaged and had to be repaired in 1919 with partial reweavings.

As well as the Gobelins tapestries, in 1918 Lever also acquired the Mortlake tapestry series depicting the story of Hero and Leander, which had been sold from Stella Hall, near Newcastle, by the family of the industrialist Sir Joseph Cowen (1800-1873). The set may have been woven for the Hall (demolished in 1955), which in the 17th century was the home of the Tempests, a wealthy Catholic courtier family, loyal throughout the reigns of the Stuart kings when the Mortlake tapestry works was at the height of its fame and production.

The Report: The Month of July, about 1730-40

French (Gobelins)

Tapestry woven in wool and silk, 425.5 x 353.5 cm

Purchased by Lever from Lews Castle, Stornoway in 1918; inv. no. LL 5203

A French copy, woven to a reduced format and in reverse, of one of the prestigious series of twelve 16th-century Brussels tapestries which use hawking, deer and boar hunting scenes to represent months of the year. The series was collectively titled *The Hunts of Maximilian* (it may originally have been produced for the Emperor Charles V) and the Lady Lever Art Gallery owns tapestries representing the months June, July and October. The copies were probably woven for an aristocrat at the court of Louis XV. The foreground hunters are making a 'report' of the animals of which they have found trace before setting off on the stag hunt. The figure on the horse to whom the hunters address their 'report' was previously thought to represent Mary of Hungary, sister of Charles V and Regent of the Low Countries, but it is now thought more likely to be her brother, Ferdinand of Austria. In the background is the Priory of Rouge-Cloître (Rooklooster), on the edge of the royal hunting forest of Soignes, south of Brussels, where the Emperor and his party often stopped during hunts.

The Meeting of Hero and Leander at the Temple of Venus, Sestos, about 1660-70

English (Mortlake)

Tapestry woven in wool and silk, 286 x 311 cm approx. (sight size)

Purchased by Lever in 1918; inv. no. LL 5464

The Gallery owns a complete set of six of one of the most popular tapestry series woven at the Thames-side Mortlake tapestry works. The works had been established in 1619 under royal patronage and made use of the weaving skills of immigrant Flemish workers. The tapestries illustrate the ancient Greek story of the tragic love of the priestess Hero for Leander. Leander swam the dangerous currents of the Hellespont, the straits between Europe and Asia at the Bosphorous, in order to see his love, but was drowned one stormy night. The series was designed by Mortlake's chief designer Francis Cleyn in 1625, and the first set was woven for James I. This set may have been woven for the Tempest family at Stella Hall from where it was sold in 1918.

The Drowning of Pharaoh in the Red Sea, about 1669-75

Damaris Pearse (1659-79)

English

Satin embroidered with silk, metal thread, mica and seed pearls in a variety of stitches and knots including long and short, split and padded detached buttonhole, 34 x 55.5 cm

Purchased by Lever in 1916; inv. no. LL 5229

An example of a skilfully embroidered raised-work picture, in which wooden moulds and wool padding were used to create a three-dimensional effect in some of the figures, while others were worked on the surface of the satin to create a sense of perspective. The picture was worked by a pious daughter of a Nonconformist minister in Devon. He published a book in memory of his daughter, *A Present for Youth and an Example for the Aged: or the Remains of Damaris Pearse,* praising her Christian virtues and her skill in 'the choicest sort of needleworks'.

Casket, 1667

British, initialled 'HP'

Canvas, satin and card faced onto a wooden casket and embroidered with silk, metal thread and seed pearls in a variety of couched threads and surface stitches including long and short, satin, brick and padded detached buttonhole, 35.6 x 29.9 x 20.5 cm

Acquired by Lever before January 1907; inv. no. LL 5256

The lid of the casket illustrates the Old Testament story of the Sacrifice of Isaac, and three scenes from the meeting of Isaac and Rebecca are shown around the sides. The front drops to reveal slim velvet-faced drawers, and the lid raises to show a typical casket interior fitted with a mirror, pincushion, bottles and other compartments, including a central mirrored well lined with a coloured Flemish print of David killing Goliath after an engraving of 1609 by Nicolas de Bruyn.

Seated Shepherdess within a Floral Border, about 1768-1800

British

Painted silk embroidered with silk in long and short, satin, stem and speckling stitches with French knots, 45 x 39.5 cm

Purchased by Lever in 1919; inv. no. LL 5380

The shepherdess may have been meant to represent Leonora, with a pet robin on her finger, from Isaac Bickerstaffe's popular comedy *The Padlock*, first performed in 1768. The fine quality of the embroidery is particularly evident in the elaborate floral border.

Gloves, about 1610-30

English

Leather with satin gauntlets, stiffened with parchment scraps, embroidered with silk in satin stitch and metal thread and trimmed with gold lace and spangles, 35 x 18 cm

Purchased by Lever in 1920; inv. no. LL 5416

The motifs embroidered on the gauntlets (the part around the wrist) - flaming hearts, eyes weeping tears and pansies representing sad thoughts - suggest that the gloves may have been intended to be presented as a love token or a *memento mori*. The gauntlets have been stiffened with parchment scraps made from reused legal documents from Norwich dating from 1602 or earlier, suggesting that the gloves date from soon afterwards.

Wedgwood

The collection of Wedgwood pottery at Lady Lever includes the world's finest array of the factory's most famous product, jasperware. The nucleus is an older collection, that of the 1st Lord Tweedmouth (1820-94), which Lever purchased in 1905. Tweedmouth in turn had bought major pieces from the naturalist Charles Darwin, whose mother Susannah was a daughter of Josiah Wedgwood. Tweedmouth was one of the first to collect 18th-century Wedgwood, beginning in the late 1840s, and he arranged his collection at his house in Inverness-shire, Guisachan, for which he also commissioned a pioneering 'Adam revival' decorative scheme in the 1850-60s from the London cabinet-makers, Wright & Mansfield.

Lever's purchase of the Tweedmouth collection turned him into a major Wedgwood collector overnight (fig. 10). The leading dealer in 'old Wedgwood' was Frederick Rathbone, and between 1905 and Rathbone's death in 1919, Lever used him to develop a thoroughly comprehensive collection. Lever was prepared to back his own judgement against that of Rathbone, notably when the dealer advised against buying the group of plaques painted by Stubbs (p. 22). Lever was buying at a time when important Victorian collections of 'old Wedgwood' were being dispersed, and wealthy Americans were entering the field. He was one of the very few British collectors of Wedgwood who had the resources to compete with them.

Josiah Wedgwood (1730-95) stands unrivalled as the greatest English potter. He not only invented and developed new types of ware, but made humble pottery fashionable, and exploited every opportunity of opening up new markets for his products. He first made his fortune in the 1760s with cream-coloured earthenware for the table, and continued to produce 'useful ware' of this kind as the bedrock of his business. At the same time he saw the potential for purely decorative 'ornamental ware' as part of the most up-to-date interior decoration. This

was far beyond the ambitions of previous Staffordshire potters.

It is easy to miss the novelty of Wedgwood's 'ornamental ware' because its classical style is now all too familiar. But it was precisely this style, based on Greek and Roman art, that made it so novel in its own time. For many Georgian connoisseurs classical art provided 'the one true style' for serious works of art, and in the 1760s Robert Adam and other architects began to adapt this style - which they called the 'antique taste' - for interior decoration. The fashion was fuelled by the publication of exciting new archaeological discoveries, notably that of the buried cities of Herculaneum and Pompeii. Greek vases, thought at that time to be not Greek but Etruscan, were dug out of tombs and lavishly illustrated in the catalogue of Sir William Hamilton's collection in 1767. Wedgwood therefore named his new factory for decorative wares 'Etruria', carefully aiming its products at the market for interior decoration in the antique taste.

To attract this market Wedgwood needed the help of someone with a thorough knowledge of up-to-date interior design and of its ancient Greek and Roman sources. Shortly before production began at Etruria in 1769, he persuaded his close friend Thomas Bentley, a cosmopolitan Liverpool merchant with a background in textile dealing, to go into partnership with him. With Bentley Wedgwood produced 'ornamental ware', while with his cousin Thomas Wedgwood he produced 'useful ware'. Bentley suggested products, briefed designers and watched London society for the latest trends to enable the firm to keep ahead of its competitors. The Lady Lever collection consists almost entirely of the 'ornamental ware' produced by Wedgwood and Bentley until the latter's death in 1780, and afterwards in the name of Wedgwood alone.

The principal products made by the partnership in its first three or four years were vases decorated to resemble

Fig. 10   Wedgwood from the Tweedmouth collection displayed at The Hill, Lever's house in Hampstead, about 1910. In Lord Tweedmouth's time most of the collection was displayed at Guisachan in Inverness-shire, but this chimneypiece was at Brook House, Park Lane. All the Wedgwood items shown here are now in the collection of the Lady Lever Art Gallery, including the Stubbs self-portrait (painted on a Wedgwood plaque) hanging above the chimneypiece (p. 22).

agate, veined marble and other stones. The shiny, glazed surface which was normal on Staffordshire earthenware was perfectly suited. But unglazed stoneware seemed more suitable for evoking the semi-matt surface of ancient pottery and the delicacy of carved reliefs, and Wedgwood spent the rest of his life perfecting different coloured stonewares of this type. First was the black, which he called 'basaltes' after the basalt rock used for sculpture. Caneware, which is cane-coloured, and 'rosso antico' ('ancient red') were also developed.

The jasperware, for which Wedgwood is famous above all else, is a white, slightly translucent stoneware (Wedgwood sometimes called it a porcelain), which could take an even tint of one of various colours. By 1774 blue and green were successful, to be followed later by lilac and yellow. Jasperware was inspired by cameo carvings in hardstones or shell, in which one colour of material is cut away around the design to reveal another background colour below. Jasperware could be made, however, on a much larger scale, and brought the delicacy of jewellery to interior decoration. Jasper was at first coloured right through the body, but Wedgwood rapidly developed the ability to achieve an even finish with a thin layer of coloured jasper over a white jasper body. This 'jasper dip' saved on the quantity of colouring agents needed for each piece. The through-coloured 'solid jasper' continued to be used for some of the best pieces where density of colour was required.

After Wedgwood's death in 1795 the factory lost its great innovative dynamo. When fashion swung away from classicism in the 1820s, the firm fell on hard times. Its fortunes were revived around the time of the Great Exhibition of 1851, but by then pioneer collectors like the future Lord Tweedmouth were already collecting 'old Wedgwood'.

The Callipygian Venus, about 1775

Black basalt, 38 x 30 cm

Purchased by Lever from Frederick Rathbone in 1916; inv. no. LL 1397

The basalt frame is integral, and the background is painted in the matt colour which Wedgwood called 'encaustic'. The figure copies an ancient statue which was very popular with visitors to Rome in the 18th century. Its title means 'with a beautiful bottom' and it was connected with a legend told by the Greek writer, Athenaeus. Two sisters solved a dispute over whose bottom was the more beautiful by asking a young man unknown to both of them to choose. His reward was the girl of his choice.

Vase, about 1775

White terracotta stoneware decorated with underglaze oxides, and gilding, 28 x 17.1 x 12.8 cm (diameter)

Purchased by Lever from the Tweedmouth collection in 1905; inv. no. LL 1018

Vases of this type were the principal product of the early years of the Wedgwood and Bentley partnership. For 20 years Staffordshire potters had imitated marble by using coloured oxides which ran in the glaze. Wedgwood's innovation was to use this technique for vases in the 'antique taste', fashionable for interior decoration. 'Terracotta stoneware' was Wedgwood's term for the type of body used here.

This vase is fixed to its plinth with a screw, and the plinth is marked 'Wedgwood and Bentley Etruria' in a circle around the screw hole. Wedgwood was the first British potter regularly to mark his wares with the name of the firm.

Vase, about 1785

Black basalt, 30.9 x 14.4 cm (diameter)

Purchased by Lever from Frederick Rathbone in 1917; inv. no. LL 1148

Wedgwood patented the matt, fired colours that he named 'encaustic', which he used on black basalt to imitate Greek red-figure vase painting. An attempt to prosecute his competitor Humphrey Palmer for infringing his patent was, however, unsuccessful. The technique was used on the 'First Day's vases', which Josiah made on the wheel on the first day of production at Etruria in 1769. It was quite different from the ancient 'encaustic' painting technique described by the Roman writer Pliny, but since there was learned controversy about this in Wedgwood's time, he chose it as a stylish brand name.

Figures of Cupid and Psyche after Etienne-Maurice Falconet (1716-1791), about 1780-1800

Black basalt, 19.9 x 10.7 x 14.5 cm and 19.9 x 10.5 x 11.7 cm

Purchased by Lever from the Tweedmouth collection in 1905; inv. nos. LL 1130 and LL 1129

The 'antique taste' made small bronze figures increasingly popular as furnishing for rooms. Wedgwood's black basalt provided a cheaper alternative which resembled bronze with a dark patina. Falconet, who was director of sculpture at the French royal porcelain factory of Sèvres, made these figures first in marble in 1757 and then in biscuit (that is, unglazed) porcelain the following year. Wedgwood may have copied them from the Sèvres version or from a plaster cast.

Chimneypiece, about 1786

Marble set with tablets of blue jasper with white jasper reliefs, 160.5 x 207.6 x 19.5 cm (depth from wall)

Purchased by Lever from Moss Harris & Sons in 1920; inv. no. LL 2643

In 1777 Wedgwood wrote that Mr Heathcote was enquiring after chimneypiece tablets for Longton Hall. This, and another similar chimneypiece in the collection, came from this house, but both are likely to date from a few years later. It was 1786 when Wedgwood wrote that he was making six chimneypieces of a new type, with even the jamb or upright panels made of jasper. The central tablet here is *The Apotheosis of Virgil* which was modelled by Flaxman as a pair to his *Apotheosis of Homer.* The three chimneypieces of this type in the Lady Lever Art Gallery are the only ones in any public collection.

Bust of Homer, about 1790

Black basalt 'bronzed' (painted), 55.7 x 30.1 x 28.4 cm

Purchased by Lever from Frederick Rathbone in 1918; inv. no. LL 1109

In 1774 Wedgwood and Bentley bought from John Cheere at Hyde Park Corner a plaster cast of a bust of Homer for l0s 6d. This was probably the origin of the present model, but its ultimate source is an ancient bust now in the National Archaeological Museum at Naples. Bronze busts were a favoured decoration for libraries, where they were ranged along the tops of bookcases. Cheere sold plaster busts not only in the white, but also painted to resemble bronze. Wedgwood used a similar technique on basalt, but the original finish has almost invariably been lost; this bust is a rare exception.

Wax relief - *Geniuses representing the Pleasures of the Elysian Fields,* 1789

Giuseppe Angelini (1742-1811)

Wax on slate, 16.5 x 40.5 mm (sight size)

Purchased by Lever from the Tweedmouth collection in 1905; inv. no. LL 2660

Between 1788 and 1790 Wedgwood commissioned some 30 wax models to be made in Rome, copying ancient relief sculptures in the Capitoline Museum. He was able to use the illustrations in a catalogue of the Museum collection as a guide. This model was made by Giuseppe Angelini copying a Roman funerary urn. (For a jasper version see the flower pot below.) The Elysian Fields were believed to be the home of the blessed in the afterlife.

Flower pot, about 1790

Lilac jasper dip with white jasper reliefs, 10.3 x 26 x 13.3 cm

Purchased by Lever from the Tweedmouth collection in 1905; inv. no. LL 1171

Lilac jasper was mentioned by Bentley in a letter to Wedgwood, but most seems to have been made after Bentley's death in 1780. The colour was difficult to control, and was therefore more commonly used for small pieces. This pair of pots for flowers or 'roots' can be dated by their relief decoration. The wax model by Giuseppe Angelini from which it is taken (see above) was received by Wedgwood in March 1790. Wedgwood was careful to distinguish between pots for holding plants and vases for the chimneypiece, which were not expected to hold anything.

Plaque - *Peace preventing Mars from opening the Door of the Temple of Janus,* about 1790

Designed by John Flaxman (1755-1826)

Solid blue jasper with white jasper reliefs, 22.8 x 25 cm (sight size)

Purchased by Lever from Frederick Rathbone in 1918; inv. no. LL 1691

Bentley selected Flaxman to model relief designs for the firm in 1775. The subject of this relief was chosen to celebrate the Commercial Treaty of 1786 with France: in ancient Rome the door of the temple of Janus was opened when war was declared. For his original wax model (now in the Wedgwood Visitor Centre at Barlaston) Flaxman was paid 15 guineas in January 1787. By this time his practice as a sculptor was flourishing, and modelling for Wedgwood was taking second place. After he left for Rome later in the year, Flaxman's work for Wedgwood was virtually over.

'Borghese' vases and pedestals, about 1790 and later

Solid blue jasper with white jasper reliefs, each vase 50.3 x 27.5 cm, each pedestal 31.5 x 26.7 cm

Purchased by Lever from the Tweedmouth collection in 1905; inv. nos. LL 1023 - 1026

These vases, the largest Josiah Wedgwood ever made in jasper, bear relief decoration following a wax model made by John Devaere in Rome in 1788. Devaere was copying the reliefs on the Borghese Vase, regarded by 18th-century critics as, with the Medici vase, one of the two finest ancient marble vases in existence. While the relief decoration of Wedgwood's vases follows closely that of the original, their form does not. The Borghese Vase is now in the Louvre in Paris.

Copy of the Portland Vase, about 1790

Solid black jasper with white jasper reliefs, 25.6 x 18.5 cm (diameter)

Purchased by Lever from the Tweedmouth collection in 1905; inv. no. LL 1204

The ancient Roman glass vase known as the Portland Vase is now in the British Museum. It was bought from the Barberini family in Rome and sold to Sir William Hamilton in 1783. Hamilton brought it to England and sold it to the Duchess of Portland. Three years later Wedgwood borrowed the vase from the Duke of Portland in order to copy it in jasper. He was a man of his time in regarding the meticulous imitation of a classical work as his finest achievement. Wedgwood's copy went on display in 1790, but probably only about 35 of this 'first edition' were made.

Cup and saucer, about 1800

Green jasper dip with white and lilac jasper reliefs,
cup 7 x 9.5 x 6.8 cm; saucer 2.4 x 12 cm (diameter)

Purchased by Lever from Frederick Rathbone in 1917;
inv. nos. LL 1333 - 1334

Jasper in three colours appears to have been in production by 1786. Wedgwood's distinction between 'ornamental' and 'useful' wares was never very watertight, and the ceramic bodies of which they were made played an important part. Anything made of jasper tended to be regarded as 'ornamental'. Jasper was used, however for the delicate little tea or coffee services for one or two persons, known as 'dejeuners', which were used by the wealthy in their dressing rooms.

Part of a tea service, about 1805

Caneware, teapot, 10.8 x 19.8 x 12.3 cm
Sugar bowl 7.5 x 12 cm (diameter)
Cup 6.4 x 10.8 x 8.9 cm (diameter)
Saucer 2.9 x 14.7 cm (diameter)

Purchased by Lever from Frederick Rathbone in 1916; inv. nos. LL 1088 - 1093

Wedgwood was making cane-coloured stoneware experimentally in 1771, but had problems with the body staining and does not seem to have been satisfied with it until some years later. The caneware body was not generally used for large tablets or vases, but was employed for figures and for vessels like plant pots. The first teaware made in it was probably that moulded to imitate bamboo canes. After Josiah's death in 1795 the caneware body was employed for a wider range of wares.

Chinese Art

Chinese porcelain was one of Lever's greatest enthusiasms as a collector, which he had already embraced by the mid-1890s and sustained to the end of his life. He particularly admired the 'blue and white' and the enamelled (mainly 'famille verte') wares of the Kangxi period (1662-1722), and it is these that dominate the Gallery's Chinese holdings. The major exception to the British concentration of the Gallery's collections, Chinese porcelain, was also a prominent feature of the collection of James Orrock, whose championing of British art so influenced Lever's own collecting. It seems that both men considered such 'china' to be an essential component of British taste in the 17th and 18th centuries and therefore suitable for a collection devoted to British art and decoration of that period. However, the taste for 'blue and white' was also an important aspect of the Aesthetic Movement at the start of Lever's collecting career, and was promoted by artists such as DG Rossetti, JAM Whistler and Frederic Leighton, as well as by other wealthy collectors.

Lever was always a conservative collector, whose taste in this field scarcely changed between the 1890s, when he began collecting Chinese porcelain for Thornton Manor (see fig. 11), and his death 30 years later. However, after deciding to establish the Lady Lever Art Gallery in 1913, he broadened the scope of his purchases to include items of more general interest: carved hardstones (see p. 104), cloisonné enamels (see p. 98), painted glass pictures (see p. 107), and Ming dynasty 'fahua' ceramics (see p. 94). But, with the exception of a Han dynasty pot bought in 1916, he ignored the new interest in early Chinese art that developed after about 1906.

Fig. 11 One end of the Music Room at Thornton Manor, 1903. Photographer Bedford Lemere. Reproduced by permission of Historic England Archive.

After Lever's death in 1925, the Trustees of the Gallery acquired a few examples of Han, Tang and Song dynasty wares in order to provide a wider-ranging view of Chinese ceramic history.

Lever's habit of buying wholesale from well-known collections was a major factor in the formation of his collection of Chinese art, a field in which he probably judged it safer to draw on the expertise of others. The most spectacular instance of this practice came in 1911 when he agreed to pay, by instalments, the substantial sum of £275,000 for the highly-regarded collection of Richard Bennett, a fellow Bolton industrialist (see pp. 97 and 102). Problems arose when Lever's supposedly secret part in the deal was leaked, and he repudiated the purchase; but after two years of legal wrangling with the dealer Edgar Gorer, Lever agreed to retain 51 items from the collection, for £55,000. Among these were

two exceptionally fine 'prunus' jars and several pieces of 'famille noire' (see p. 101-2) - two types of porcelain that had become highly fashionable and exceedingly expensive. While prestige must have had a lot to do with Lever's interest in the Bennett collection, after 1913 this type of 'bulk buying' became a convenient way of acquiring for his museum representative selections of good quality objects that lay outside his main area of interest. So, all his jade carvings and cloisonné enamels came from just two sources: the famous collection of Sir Trevor Lawrence (in 1916; see p. 104) and that of Lord Wharncliffe (in 1920). Other collections from which Lever bought quantities of Chinese art were those of Sydney E Kennedy (see pp. 94 and 101) Alfred W Stiff (see p. 98), Robert H Benson and, in 1903 and 1904, James Orrock (Lever's later bulk-purchases from Orrock included very little Chinese material).

Vase

Ming dynasty (1488-1505)

Southern China, Hongzhi reign

Porcelain enamelled on the biscuit in the 'fahua' style, 42 x 27 cm

Purchased by Lever from the Sydney E Kennedy sale, 1916; inv. no. LL 6067 (X 1529)

The 'fahua' style of ceramics was produced in China from the 14th to 16th centuries and may well have been intended as a less expensive substitute for cloisonné enamels. The bold designs on this type of pot are outlined with threads of clay; after firing, the outlined areas are filled in with a limited range of coloured glazes. The origin of the term 'fahua' is uncertain but it may mean 'Buddhist decoration' and derive from the fact that these wares were very often used in Buddhist temples. This vase features the so-called Eight Immortals of the Wine Cup, a group of poets of the Tang dynasty (618-906) 'immortalised' in the work of the poet Du Fu (712-770) and as famous for their drunkenness as for their verse. Their faces have been left unglazed and they are identified by the wine jars on which they lean.

Figure of Guanyin
(Goddess of Mercy)

**Ming dynasty, Chenghua reign
(1465-1487), 1484**

Liu Zhen

Northern China

Stoneware with coloured glazes,
140 x 73.3 x 48 cm

Purchased by the 2nd Viscount
Leverhulme, about 1937, then
presented to the Gallery by the 3rd
Viscount Leverhulme, 1980;
inv. no. LL 6000

Guanyin is the Chinese (and normally
female) manifestation of the
Buddhist Bodhisattva of compassion,
Avalokitesvara. Bodhisattvas are
beings who have reached Nirvana
(Enlightenment) but who choose
to stay in the world to help others
achieve the same. An inscription on
this figure tells us that it was the gift
of a man named Dang and his wife
Chong, dedicated on an auspicious
mid-autumn day in 1484 under the
supervision of the priest Daoji. It
belongs to a group of at least four
different figures from the same
unknown northern Chinese temple,
all dedicated on the same occasion
and inscribed with the maker's name,
Liu Zhen. The group, now split up
between various British museums,
appears to have been taken from China
in the 1930s, when the 2nd Viscount
Leverhulme (and not his father)
acquired the Guanyin.

Two figures of K'uei Hsing (Kui Xing)

(left) Ming dynasty (1368-1644), about 1600-44

Porcelain with coloured glazes, 30.5 x 22.1 x 10.7cm

Purchased by Lever, 1916; inv. no. LL 6134 (X 1697)

(right) Qing dynasty, Kangxi reign (1662-1722), about 1662-1700

Porcelain enamelled on the biscuit in 'famille verte' colours, 32 x 22.2 x 11.5 cm

Purchased by Lever, 1915; inv. no. LL 61 (X 442)

In Chinese popular religion, Kui Xing is the patron of students who awards success in examinations. Standing on a fish-dragon, he holds up a writing brush in his right hand and an inkstone in his left. He is said to have been an historical figure, a poor but brilliant student called Zhong Kui who passed the imperial examinations with high honours. However, because he was repulsively ugly (as these figures show), he was not allowed to enter government service. In despair, he drowned himself but was carried by a fish-dragon up to heaven where he became a star ('xing' in Chinese) in the Great Bear constellation (known in China as the Palace of Literary Genius). Although these two figures are closely similar in form, the one on the right, decorated in the 'famille verte' manner, was made somewhat later than the one on the left.

Wine ewer

**Qing dynasty, Kangxi reign
(1662-1722), about 1662-1700**

Porcelain enamelled on the biscuit in
'famille verte' colours, 22.6 x 20.4 x 5.6 cm

Purchased by Lever from the Richard
Bennett collection, 1911-13;
inv. no. LL 24 (RB 283)

This ewer is modelled in the form of
the character 'shou', meaning 'long life'.
The panels on each side underline this
symbolism. On one side can be seen four
symbols of longevity: a pine tree, a crane,
a deer and the sacred 'lingzhi' fungus. On
the other side (shown here) two cranes are
flying towards a pavilion.

Peach-shaped wine pot

Ming dynasty, 17th century

Porcelain with coloured glazes,
15.7 x 17.3 x 10.5cm

Purchased by Lever from the Alfred W Stiff sale,
1916; inv. no. LL 23 (X 1680)

The peach is an important symbol of long life,
sacred to the Daoist goddess Xiwang Mu (the
Queen Mother of the West). The peaches of
longevity grow in her garden in the Kunlun
Mountains and are the main delicacy at her
birthday banquets. Hence, peaches are
commonly found in association with birthday
gifts and are popular among Daoists, for
whom the quest for immortality is of central
importance. This type of wine pot, which has no
lid and is filled through a hole in the base, was
copied by several English potters in the form
of 'Cadogan' teapots, which were particularly
popular in the years around 1830.

Beaker

**Ming dynasty, probably Wanli reign
(1573-1620), about 1600**

Cloisonné enamel on copper, 56.3 x 39.9 x 39.8 cm

Purchased by Lever from the Alfred W Stiff sale,
1916; inv. no. LL 5901 (X 1486)

After Chinese connoisseurs began to collect archaic bronze vessels in the Tang dynasty (618-906), it became common to imitate bronze forms in other materials. The form of this vessel is not genuinely archaic but is made to appear so by the addition of four cast ribs to the sides. The beaker is one of a pair and would originally have been accompanied by an incense burner and two candlesticks to form a temple altar set. The Buddhist decoration of scrolling lotus flowers symbolises Enlightenment. The cloisonné enamel technique involves soldering a pattern of wires onto a metal surface, then filling the enclosed areas (cloisons) with enamel colours which are fired and polished to create a smooth, sparkling surface. On the base of this beaker is a Jingtai reign mark (1450-6), paying homage to what the Chinese consider to have been the classic period for this art form. Although technical perfection was achieved in the Qing dynasty (1644-1911), the bolder forms and richer colours of the earlier period compare favourably with the fussier, more glittery style of the 18th and 19th centuries.

Dish

Qing dynasty, Kangxi reign (1662-1722), about 1700-22

Porcelain enamelled over the glaze in 'famille verte' colours, with some gilding, 3.5 x 26.7 cm

Acquired by Lever before June 1907; inv. no. LL 68 (H 283)

Three heroes of 'The Water Margin', the popular novel written in the 16th century by Shi Nai'an, are identified by the names on their belts: (left to right) Chai Jin, Song Jiang and Yan Qing. The figures are probably based on illustrations of the novel made by Chen Hongshou in the 1640s and 1650s. Similar dishes with different heroes exist in other collections. Although the dish was made during the Kangxi reign, it has on the base a mark of the Chenghua reign (1465-87). This mark is not intended to deceive but to show respect for the excellent ceramics of the earlier period; it is also a sign that the dish was made by a non-imperial factory.

Plate

Qing dynasty, Kangxi reign (1662-1722), about 1662-1700

Porcelain enamelled over the glaze in 'famille verte' colours, with some gilding, 5.4 x 37.6 cm

Acquired by Lever before June 1907; inv. no. LL 32 (H 15)

Two mounted warriors are shown engaged in combat; this is perhaps an historical subject derived from a contemporary illustrated book. The rim decoration includes medallions containing cranes, emblems of long life, while on the back, the plate has flowers painted over an incised petal pattern. There are two marks: a non-imperial factory mark of an artemisia leaf (an auspicious plant said to drive away diseases) and a later engraved mark of the collection of Augustus the Strong, Elector of Saxony. Presumably the plate was once displayed in the Japanese Palace built for Augustus in Dresden between 1729 and 1737. Augustus was a notoriously extravagant collector of east Asian porcelain; on one occasion he is said to have given away a whole regiment of dragoons in exchange for twelve Chinese vases.

Pair of vases

Qing dynasty, Kangxi reign (1662-1722)

Porcelain enamelled over the glaze in 'famille verte' colours, 43.8 x 20.9 cm

Acquired by Lever before June 1907; inv. nos. LL 28, LL 6110 (H 240)

These vases depict the 'Four Elegant Accomplishments', cultural pursuits traditionally considered to be appropriate for women of leisure and scholars. On one vase, Painting is represented by three women looking at a picture scroll and Literature by a woman reading at a table. The other vase features Games (women playing checkers) and Music (a woman playing a 'qin', a zither-like stringed instrument). The landscapes round the neck are probably the work of a different specialist painter. On the base of each vase is painted a sacred fungus; this is the mark of a private, non-imperial factory and expresses a wish for long life.

Candle-holder

Qing dynasty, Kangxi reign (1662-1722)

Porcelain enamelled over the glaze in 'famille noire' and 'famille verte' colours, 41 x 26.2 x 16.3 cm

Purchased by Lever from the Sydney E Kennedy sale, 1916; inv. no. LL 6131 (X 1550)

A young African woman holds in her right hand a horn-shaped candle socket. Her elaborate jewellery includes real pearl earrings, a star-shaped ornament on her forehead and a sash of flowers. By the time that this unusual figure was made the Chinese had been familiar with Africans for many centuries; there were African slaves in China as early as the Tang dynasty (618-906), and between 1405 and 1433 seven major maritime expeditions, led by the Muslim eunuch Zheng He, had reached the east coast of Africa. By the Kangxi period a large African community was established in the Portuguese settlement at Macao. Lever's collection contains another similar candle-holder bought on a separate occasion.

Vase

Probably Qing dynasty, Kangxi reign (1662-1722)

Porcelain enamelled on the biscuit in 'famille noire' colours, 76.2 x 27.1 cm

Acquired by Lever before June 1907;
inv. no. LL 6130 (H 259)

Lever insured this vase for £10,000, a reflection of the fact that 'famille noire' became, in the 1910s and '20s, the most sought-after and expensive porcelain in the world. Although these wares are usually rather crudely decorated, prices shot up to unprecedented levels. It is now suspected that much of the 'famille noire' sold at this time was either faked or produced by adding a black ground to genuine 'famille verte' items. Lever himself was aware of this problem and always preferred to examine pieces in person before buying. It has been suggested that pieces of 'famille noire' as big as this could not have been made as early as the Kangxi reign, but this vase does in fact seem to be a genuine early example. It has a Chenghua reign mark (1465-87), a sign that it was made by a non-imperial factory.

Jar and lid

Qing dynasty, Kangxi reign (1662-1722), about 1700

Porcelain with underglaze blue decoration, 26.2 x 21.8 cm

Purchased by Lever from the Richard Bennett collection, 1911-13; inv. no. LL 72 (RB 1)

'Prunus' jars like this became an obsession of British and American collectors in the late 1890s, and by 1905 could sell for up to £6,000 each. Connoisseurs paid attention to the perfection of the azure blue colour and, according to those standards, this example of Lever's has been considered the finest in any western collection. The jars were used in China as containers for gifts of tea or other delicacies at the lunar New Year Festival in January or February. Appropriately, the design celebrates the approach of spring: branches of prunus blossom (which appears in late winter) are depicted against a background of cracking ice.

Vase

**Qing dynasty, Kangxi reign (1662-1722),
about 1700-22**

Porcelain with underglaze blue decoration, enamelled
over the glaze in 'famille verte' colours, with gilding,
43.8 x 19.4 cm

Acquired by Lever before June 1907; inv. no. LL 93
(H 289)

Lever was clearly enthusiastic about the unusual
'powder blue' technique, and this vase is just one
example from the large collection he formed. The
speckled ground was produced by blowing powdered
cobalt oxide onto the unglazed pot through a bamboo
tube with gauze over the end. The reserved white areas
on this vase were masked by paper patches, applied in
the slapdash manner often found on work intended for
export. The white panels were then painted in 'famille
verte' colours (fixed by a second low-temperature
firing) with a design of black-backed finches sitting on
prunus branches. The gilded design of plants, birds and
insects on the blue ground has survived unusually well,
considering how easily such gilding is rubbed off.

Vase and lid

Qing dynasty, Qianlong reign (1736-95)

Porcelain with underglaze blue decoration; 31.8 x 15.9 cm

Acquired by Lever before June 1907; inv. no. LL 26 (H 159)

This vase was made at a time when blue and white porcelain
was out of fashion in China. Nevertheless, it displays a lively and
imaginative sense of design, with the gourds in the decoration
neatly echoing the overall form of the vase. The double-gourd
shape is a traditional Chinese form not usually found in wares
made for export, suggesting that this vase may have been
intended for the Chinese domestic market.

Garniture of three lidded vases and two beakers

Qing dynasty, Kangxi reign (1662-1722), about 1662-1700

Porcelain with underglaze blue decoration, (left to right) 54.5 x 20.5 cm, 48.9 x 23.7 cm, 55.9 x 20.5 cm, 48.7 x 23.5 cm and 54.9 x 20.7cm

Purchased by Lever from the George Salting sale, 1900; inv. nos. LL 96-100 (H 53)

Blue and white groups of this sort decorated the walls, mantelpieces and furniture of wealthy Europeans in vast numbers from at least the middle of the 17th century. Lever followed firmly in this tradition and this garniture is typical of his personal taste. In the West, the design has been called the 'rose and ticket' pattern after the flowers round the sides and the ticket-like oval medallions round the rims or shoulders.

Vase and lid

Qing dynasty, Qianlong reign (1736-95)

Jade (nephrite), 35.6 x 23 x 8.5 cm

Purchased by Lever from the Sir Trevor Lawrence sale, 1916; inv. no. LL 70 (X 1425)

Made from one piece of jade, this vase displays the great virtuosity achieved by the best jade-carvers of the Qing dynasty; it may even have been made for imperial use. Jade is too hard to be cut with steel tools and therefore must be ground with abrasive sands and water, down to the smallest detail; a slow and very demanding process. In Chinese culture jade has always been more highly esteemed than gold, not only because the main source is far away in Central Asia but also because of the spiritual qualities it is believed to embody. This vase is an altar vessel, and around the edge of each side bears the eight Buddhist Auspicious Signs:

(clockwise from the top) the Umbrella, the Paired Fish, the Vase, the Lotus Flower, the Conch Shell, the Endless Knot, the Banner of Victory, and the Dharma Wheel (the wheel of Buddhist law, symbolising the unity of all things).

Altar ornament

Qing dynasty, Qianlong reign (1736-95)

Porcelain enamelled over the glaze in 'famille rose' colours, with jade, coral and ivory, 70.6 x 63.6 x 39.8 cm

Purchased by Lever, 1920; inv. no. LL 6133 (X 3830/1)

One of a pair of Buddhist altar ornaments in the form of an elaborately-dressed elephant. The elephant is a Chinese symbol of peace and, in Buddhist thought, is ridden by the Bodhisattva Samantabhadra.

A vase on its back is a symbolic container for the three sacred Buddhist jewels - the Buddha, the Dharma (the Buddha's teachings) and the Sangha (the community of practising Buddhists). The vase on this elephant is painted to imitate a cloisonné enamel altar vessel and contains leaves of jade with berries of coral.

Vase

Qing dynasty, Qianlong reign (1736-95)

Porcelain enamelled over the glaze in 'famille rose' colours, 35.5 x 15.8 cm

Acquired by Lever before June 1907;
inv. no. LL 6060 (H 325)

This finely-potted vase, with its elegant shape and carefully-arranged design of peonies and a tree in blossom, is a good example of the sophisticated wares produced at this period for the Chinese domestic market. It is in marked contrast to the increasingly crowded decoration to be found on contemporary export wares. On the base is a Qianlong reign mark painted in red enamel, its characters in the form normally used on seals. Because the mark refers to the reign during which the vase was made, it is possible that it was produced by an imperial factory.

Glass picture of a shepherdess and falconer

Probably painted in Guangzhou (Canton), Qing dynasty, Qianlong reign (1736-95), about 1760

Painted and mirrored glass, 55.3 x 43.2 cm

Purchased by Lever, 1918; inv. no. LL 8805 (X 2434)

Pictures of this sort, painted on the back of glass and then mirrored, were originally produced only for export to Europe. Because China itself could not produce glass of high enough quality, the glass panels were shipped there from Europe to be painted in the workshops of the Guangzhou area. Templates were used to produce series of nearly identical paintings. The pictures contain traditional Chinese features (in this example, the river and mountains as key elements in the landscape), but they are painted in a Western manner heavily influenced by European prints sent to China for copying. The falconer and shepherdess figures reflect European ideas and fashions of the time, not Chinese taste. For wealthy Europeans, China was a fantastically exotic place and rural life was romantic and full of pleasure; for the Chinese, falconry and sheep-herding are barbaric activities associated with the nomads of the Mongolian grasslands. This painting appears to have retained its original carved and gilt Chinese frame.

Greek and Roman Antiquities

Lever became a serious collector of antiquities only after deciding to found the Lady Lever Art Gallery in June 1913; indeed only one item in the Gallery's collection, a Roman altar from the Capel-Cure sale of 1905, was purchased before that date. It is likely that he formed the collection for educational reasons and, in particular, he was also concerned to show the prime sources for English neo-classical art, and especially for his collection of Wedgwood pottery.

Lever began acquiring antiquities almost immediately, when he bought six Greek vases and a Roman bust at the Stafford House sale in July 1913 (p. 67). Two years later he was a purchaser at the sales of Jeffery Whitehead (buying four Greek vases) and of CTD Crews of Billingbear Park (five Greek vases and two Roman funerary urns). His two greatest opportunities came in 1917. In that year he bought from the dealer Moss Harris 27 vases and a few terracotta figurines that had been in the collection of Alexander Ionides (1840-1898). Lever was the largest purchaser at Christie's sale of the collection formed by Thomas Hope (1769-1831), the most important group of antiquities to come on the market for generations. At the sale Lever bought 35 ancient vases and sculptures, as well as the late 18th-century group of Cephalus and Aurora, which was bought by Hope from John Flaxman when the latter was working in Rome (p. 23).

In common with the majority of collections originally formed in the 18th and 19th centuries, the precise archaeological find-spots for the Greek painted pottery and most of the Roman sculpture in Lever's collection are not known. The majority of the Greek vases which Lever acquired at the sale of Thomas Hope's antiquities were originally part of the second collection formed in Naples by Sir William Hamilton, and had escaped the shipwreck of the *Colossus* on its journey from Naples to England. By contrast, some of the Greek vases which Lever purchased from Alexander Ionides' collection, were almost certainly acquired in Greece.

Lever's collection of Greek and Roman antiquities predominantly covers Greek painted pottery and Roman sculpture. Other forms of Greek and Roman art, such as terracotta figurines, Greek sculpture or Roman mosaics, are either barely represented or not at all. Notwithstanding, Lever's collection of Greek painted pottery includes examples of the output of Athenian, Corinthian, Lakonian, South Italian and Etrusco-Corinthian workshops dating from the 7th to the 4th centuries BC, many from identifiable individuals or workshops. The Roman sculpture at the Lady Lever Art Gallery includes examples of marble sculptures dating from the 1st and 2nd centuries AD. 'The collection's main importance derives from the preservation of the largest part of the collection of ancient sculpture assembled by Thomas Hope still surviving in the UK. Fourteen of the sculptures on display in the Gallery are from the Hope collection, including the sculpture of Antinous which stands in the north rotunda

Antique and later sculpture in the Gallery's North Rotunda. © Pete Carr

Oinochoe (wine jug),
about 625-600 BC

The Bearded Sphinx Painter

Etruscan

Pottery, 28.9 x 16.1 x 15.6 cm (diameter)

Purchased by Lever from the Ionides
collection in 1917; inv. no. LL 5063

The oinochoe was used to dip into a bowl of
wine to pour into cups. It is decorated using
a technique called black-figure; the figures
were painted in a slip which fired glossy
black, with details incised. Although it was
made in an Etruscan workshop in central
Italy, the style of decoration imitated
pottery made in Corinth. The name of the
painter of this vessel is unknown, although
he or she is called the Bearded Sphinx
Painter, named after their practice of
painting sphinxes with beards.

Psykter (wine cooler), about 525-500 BC

Greek, from Athens

Pottery, 33.5 x 25 cm (diameter)

Purchased by Lever from the Hope Heirlooms sale
in 1917; inv. no. LL 5034

This unusually shaped vessel is called a psykter,
and it was used to cool wine, either by placing the
psykter in a bowl of ice and filling it with wine,
or vice versa. The decoration, in the black-figure
technique, is appropriate to the vessel's function,
as it shows the Greek god Dionysos, god of wine,
accompanied by his companions.

Roman

Marble, 52.7 x 49.8 x 45.2 cm

Purchased by Lever from the Hope Heirlooms sale in 1917; inv. no. LL 11

During the 1st and 2nd centuries AD, cremation was the favoured burial practice in the Roman Empire, which led to the production of ash chests (cineraria) to contain the remains of the deceased. This cinerarium was made to contain the ashes of Caius Perperna Geminus, who died aged 68. It was dedicated by his heirs Caius Perperna Agathopus, Saturnina and Fortunata, all of whom had been slaves. The cinerarium was said to have been discovered in a tomb in Siena in the early 18th century and was later bought by sculptor Bartolomeo Cavaceppi, who is likely to have been responsible for its restoration. The ash chest came from the Thomas Hope collection, having been purchased from Lord Bessborough in 1801.

Amphora, about 510-500 BC

Greek, from Athens

Pottery, 39.9 x 26.2 cm (diameter)

Purchased by Lever from the Hope Heirlooms sale in 1917; inv. no. LL 5014

The term amphora is used to describe a two-handled pot with a neck narrower than the body, designed for the storage and transport of liquids and solid commodities such as grain. Decorated amphoras were often found in Etruscan tombs, exported from Athenian workshops. This amphora, decorated in the black-figure technique, shows a rider, flanked by two warriors. The painter used a frontal pose for the horse and rider, possibly to demonstrate his or her expertise, although to modern eyes it is not wholly successful.

Krater (mixing bowl), about 500-475 BC

Greek, from Athens

Pottery, 34.4 x 35.8 x 31 cm (diameter)

Purchased by Lever from the Hope Heirlooms sale in 1917; inv. no. LL 5035

The krater was used for mixing water with wine. The decoration on this vessel is very appropriate, as it shows young male revellers on one side and Dionysos and a satyr (one of his male companions) on the other; both images related to the Greek symposium, a social occasion at which wine was drunk. The krater is decorated using a technique called red-figure; the background was painted in a slip which fired glossy black, with the figures left in the reddish-brown colour of the clay. Details within the figures were painted rather than engraved, leading to painters attempting more ambitious poses than previously, such as the twisting stance of the three young men on the krater.

DIS MANIB C PER PERNA
C F SER GEMINO C PER PER
ACATHOPVS ET SATVRNINA
ET FORTVNATA H
LIB FEC V A LXVIII

L LAC II

Roman

Marble, 118.6 x 50.6 x 37.8 cm

Purchased by Lever from the Hamilton Palace sale in 1919; inv. no. LL 8

This table support in the form of a lion came from the collection of the Duke of Hamilton at Hamilton Palace, South Lanarkshire. The base and the table top are mid-17th-century restorations. The Gallery has another example of the same form, but in baroque style, which may have been made at the same time as this antique example was restored; it too was in the Hamilton Palace collection.

Candelabrum, 1st century AD

Roman

Marble, 246 x 49 cm (diameter)

Purchased by Lever from the Hope Heirlooms sale in 1917; inv. no. LL 16

This candelabrum was extensively restored in the late 18th century to satisfy contemporary taste for 'complete' works of art: the ancient elements on which it is based - the main shaft below the rams' heads and part of the base - would not have been acceptable as fragments. The restoration is very much in the style of the sculptor and engraver Giambattista Piranesi (1720-1778), but the history of this piece is unknown before 1804 when it was first recorded in Thomas Hope's collection.

Statue of Antinous, about AD 130-8

Roman

Marble, 232.5 x 69 x 91 cm

Purchased by Lever from the Hope Heirlooms sale in 1917; inv. no. LL 208

Antinous, a youth of renowned beauty from Bithynia in north-west Asia Minor (modern-day Turkey), was the Emperor Hadrian's lover, and was deified after drowning himself in the Nile in AD 130. This statue, one of many carved after his death, is likely to have been based on a Classical Greek prototype of the 5th century BC. The statue was restored in the late 18th century by the sculptor Pierantoni, whose additions include the cup and the jug.

Saddle and harness, 1812 and later

Japan

Lacquered and partly gilt hardwood, iron, iron inlaid with silver, painted and gilt leather, dyed hemp(?) string, gilt paper strip, basketry, wool, linen and silk.

Inv. no. LL 8416 - 8423

Saddles like this were for ceremonial use rather than for battle. An inscription on the underside of the lacquered wood saddle records that it was made for a man called Fukugimi by Bangiko (?) Morifumi (from Ingebouri Prefecture, of Ise Province), and later restored by Sadafumi.

Lever purchased the saddle from Harishin, 'Collector of Fine Art Curios' at Kobe. It was said that, 'This Harness had been used by a warrior ("Samurai") call [sic] Katayama Goneman who belong [sic] to Kochi Daimio or chief of Josa province, 250 years ago. At the time of restration [sic] it sold away with furnitures'.

The Ethnography Collection

Mr WH Lever, who in his travels round the world has had ample opportunity to gratify his taste as a collector.[1]

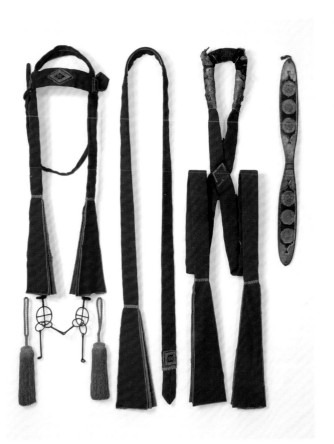

Before his death in 1925 Lever had assembled an eclectic and very personal collection of objects that reflected his travels around the world. The ethnographic or 'museum' collection he amassed included over 1,000 objects from across Africa, the Pacific Islands, North America and parts of Asia. He embraced everything from 40 foot-long war canoes made in the Solomon Islands (and at one stage stored in the Port Sunlight bicycle shed) to tiny gold weights from Ghana. Although it is not quite so evident today, this was a large and important part of Lever's collecting strategy and the ethnographic collection was intended to have a starring role in the new displays designed for the Lady Lever Art Gallery, which would open in December 1922.

Business, collecting and 'round the world' trips

They [the islanders of Samoa] all crowded round the ship in their canoes, offering for sale corals, shells, native cloth, pine apples, bananas, etc. [2]

Lever's ethnographic collecting and his business ventures were inextricably tied to each other. It is highly likely that Lever's first world trip from September 1892 to March 1893, which took him across North America and from there to Hawai'i, Samoa, New Zealand, Australia and Sri Lanka, sparked his passion for ethnographic objects. Lever never just travelled for pleasure and it was his business ventures that brought him to the places where he collected. A lack of diaries and collecting notes make it difficult to say with any degree of certainty what he actually collected during his early trips, but we do know that this tour of the Pacific signalled his expansion into the southern hemisphere with his first Australian soap factory.

More overseas tours followed, with Australia and South Africa in 1895-96 and a second world tour in 1901. The 1901 trip was a significant one for Lever. It was during this tour that his commercial interests in the Pacific began, and records show that he was collecting as he travelled. He purchased, amongst other things, bags, a comb, a shark's jaw (for £6) and 'two idols' (for £5) from a trader in Sydney, Australia.

By 1904 Lever had started to think about developing his opportunistically amassed ethnographic souvenirs into a more systematic collection. As in other areas of his collecting life, Lever looked to supplement his existing objects with ready made ethnographic collections, particularly from the Pacific Islands, which was a place of great commercial interest to him. He was offered several Pacific collections during this time including, 'a collection of curios from the South Seas for our Museum... and in view of our connection in the South Seas I am disposed to look further into the matter'[3]. Despite it containing 600 objects and a collection catalogue he decided to turn it down. He would go on to acquire two full-size canoes from the Solomon Islands in 1913, but by this time his collecting and business interests had already turned to Africa.

The period 1911-14 was a time of development for both Lever's ethnographic collection and his business interests in Africa, specifically in the Congo. Having been blocked from buying up land for his palm oil ventures in British-controlled areas of West Africa, Lever turned his attentions to the Belgian-controlled Congo. Here, he was able to take advantage of the cheap palm oil concessions and he negotiated the continued use of enforced local labour. This was also a time of considerable collecting. During his Congo tour of 1912-13 he was given collections by missionaries, and he also appears to have tried to purchase objects directly from their owners, although his tour diaries show he was not always successful.

Just four months after his return from the Congo, Lever's wife died. Almost immediately he embarked on another world tour which would again take him across North America and then to Japan, China, Hong Kong, the Philippine Islands, New Guinea, the Solomon Islands, New Zealand and Australia. This tour inevitably included inspection tours of his plantations and factories, but it also resulted in the acquisition of some of Lever's most iconic ethnographic objects, including a samurai saddle, purchased from a dealer in Kobe, Japan and a very fine drum used by the Ojibwa Nation, which he purchased

in Calgary. It was also during this trip that he purchased an impressive war canoe (now in the British Museum). By 1922 Lever's collection included textiles from Sierra Leone, a Chinese divination compass, saddles and trappings from Mexico, First Nations dress and textiles, and a collection of gold weights from Ghana purchased from a fellow collector.

Lever made further world tours in both 1923-24 and 1924-25, which included the Congo and involved more collecting. In fact, he continued to acquire objects until his death in 1925. His ethnographic collection was at the forefront of his public exhibition and education programme on Merseyside for almost 20 years.

Displaying the 'museum' collection

Revds Mr Forfeitt and Mr Maines came to see us and brought curiosities &c, for our Port Sunlight Museum.[4]

As the name suggests the 'museum' collection was brought together with display in mind. More than 400 objects were already in the collection by 1903 when Lever's first displays opened at the Free Library and Museum, the home of Lever's first museum in Port Sunlight. A visitor to this early exhibition would have seen objects and weapons from across the Pacific, especially the Solomon Islands, and a number of personal ornaments from South Africa. By 1911 the 'museum' collection had outgrown its first home and was transferred to Hulme Hall, which had once been a factory canteen for girls. Yet again the majority of the items on display were ethnographic with displays entitled 'Nigeria' and 'Congo'. Now the museum visitor could see an eclectic mix of textiles, barkcloths, masks, feasting bowls (described as washing tubs) and even more weapons, predominately from across central and southern Africa and the Pacific Islands. Juxtaposed alongside these were soap specimens, crimping irons and steel samples.

With the end of the First World War in 1918 the well-developed plans for a new museum could be resurrected. These plans would become the Lady Lever Art Gallery. In the year prior to the new gallery's opening, Lever considered the displays with his Assistant Curator, Mr AC Tait. At this stage, there was every intention of showing the full range of his collection in the new gallery, and the African and Pacific ethnography would sit alongside European paintings, sculpture and furniture. Lever even asked Tait to move the Chinese porcelain to make room for, 'West African and Solomon Island curios',[5] the intention being that these objects would occupy the balcony galleries (now Room 10).

Despite the years of dedicated collecting and the careful planning it was not to be, and it is still unclear why Lever made the final decision to take his collection of ethnography out of his new gallery plans. It may have been a consequence of changing attitudes to ethnographic objects at that time, or just as likely, his decision may have been influenced by the disastrous takeover of the Niger Company. His business deals and his collecting programmes were never far apart, and his ethnography collection may have been just too powerful a reminder of all that he had relinquished as a result of this unwise business venture that nearly bankrupted his company. Whatever the reason for this change of heart, Lever moved much of his ethnographic collection to Lever Brothers' new London headquarters in 1922, where it would be displayed as a symbol of the company's worldwide influence. Following his death in 1925, Lever's collection of ethnography was split up and either sold or given away. Just a small part of this 'museum' collection now remains at the Lady Lever Art Gallery.

The Lever ethnography collection that is still part of the Lady Lever Art Gallery offers a glimpse of what once was. The objects that remain reflect Lever's business interests and his worldwide and colonial connections. They also remind us that Lever's passion for collecting was as expansive as his business interests and was not just limited to art. Lever always intended his ethnographic objects, collected during business ventures and world tours, to be viewed alongside his other 'art' collections, but a last minute decision changed both this and our perception of Lever as a collector.

1 Progress [Lever Brothers House Magazine] October 1903, p.374. Cited in A West (1992).

2 WH Lever Following the Flag. Jottings of a jaunt round the world 1893, p. 62. Cited in A West (1992)

3 LLAG, letter, Lever to Pacific Islands Co. Ltd., 9 November 1904, file 3947. Cited in A West (1992).

4 Unilever information library, London. TT3810 Lever's Tour Diary, Congo 1912-13. Cited in A West (1992).

5 Tait Business Correspondence, Lady Lever Art Gallery Archives. Cited in A West (1996)

Carved staff, late 19th century
Solomon Islands
Wood, shell and metal
Inv. no. LL 8673

The people of the Solomon Islands decorated all the things that they most valued, from feasting bowls to ceremonial staffs. Objects of status and authority were always highly decorated with the time-consuming technique of inlaying. Contrasting pieces of nautilus shell, with the dark smooth contours of the wood, created objects of immense beauty that were readily collected by foreigners who arrived on the islands' shores.

The staff in Lever's collection was likely made for the tourist trade as the shell decoration is not as fine as that seen on an object that an islander would make for his own community.

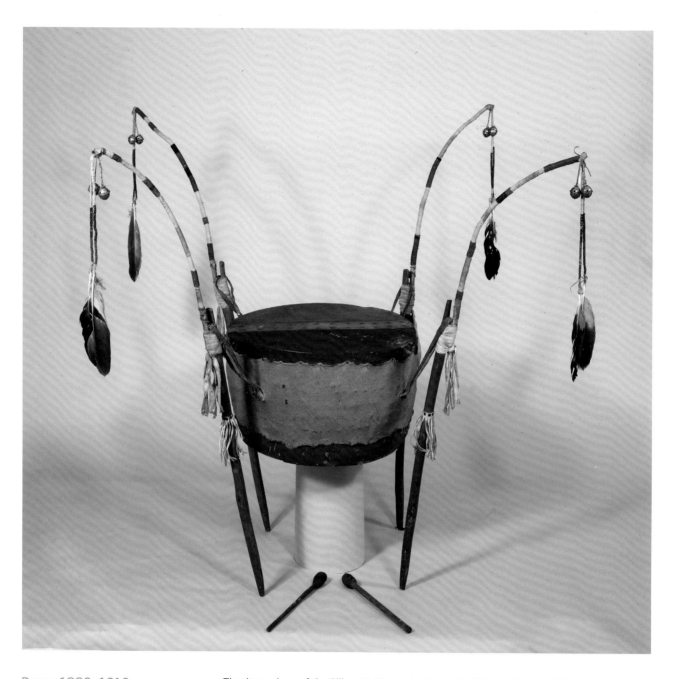

Drum, 1880 -1910

Ojibwa Nation

North America (Western Great Lakes),

Painted wood, rawhide, textile, beads, metal and feathers.

Inv. no. LL 8400-8406

The dance drum of the Ojibwa Nation and other central Algonquian-speaking peoples came into use around 1880, partly in response to the new non- nomadic lifestyle forced upon them after they were settled in reservations. It was the focus of ceremonial dances performed by drum societies, which were intended to promote peace. A new drum society could be initiated by the gift of a drum from an existing society to another community, and all claimed ultimate 'descent' from the original drum made following a revelation to a prophetess of the Sioux Nation.

Lever bought the drum, along with eagle feather bonnets, moccasins and a child's dress, from Mackay and Dippie Ltd, fur dealers and taxidermists in Calgary during his 1913 trip.

Ikhoko pendants, late 19th century

Pende People

Bandundu Province, South Central Democratic Republic of Congo

Ivory

Inv. nos. LL 8042-8043

Pende sculptors carved miniature ivory replicas of mbuya initiation society masks. The replicas were worn as pendants by close members of the mask keeper's family to protect them from the spiritual dangers associated with his work. Mbuya masks drew their power from ancestral spirits and could be used to heal sickness. A person cured with the help of an mbuya mask might wear an ikhoko pendant to prolong the mask's curative influence.

Fig. 12   Leverville, one of the model
villages Lever developed from 1911;
photographed 1924-5. Reproduced
with kind permission of Unilever from
an original in Unilever Archives.

WILLIAM HESKETH. FIRST VISCOUNT LEVERHULME
1851 — 1925
AS JUNIOR GRAND WARDEN OF ENGLAND
GEORGE HALL NEALE

William Hesketh Lever,
Baron Leverhulme of
Bolton-le-Moors, as
Junior Grand Warden
of England, 1918

**George Hall Neale
(1863-1940)**

British

Oil on canvas, 213.8 x 120 cm

Transferred from Lever's
private collection, 1922,
inv. no. LL 3747